ABCs of
Longarm
Quilting

Patricia C. Barry

©2007 Patricia C. Barry
Published by

kp **krause publications**
An Imprint of F+W Publications

700 East State Street • Iola, WI 54990-0001
715-445-2214 • 888-457-2873
www.krausebooks.com

Our toll-free number to place an order or obtain
a free catalog is (800) 258-0929.

The following registered trademark terms and companies appear in this publication:
Gammill, Statler Stitcher, Snake Light, Signature, Madeira, Sulky, A&E, Inc.,
Euro-notions, The Stencil Co., Heritage, Golden Threads.

Library of Congress Catalog Number: 2006935646

ISBN: 978-0-89689-454-9

Edited by Andy Belmas
Designed by Emily Adler

Printed in China

Introduction

This book is written for anyone who is contemplating getting into longarm quilting and for those of you who have purchased a quilting system and now are looking for more detail.

I became a professional quilter when I opened my studio in 2002. My original business proposition was to start a retail quilting studio. I wanted to teach people to use my longarm quilting machines so they could finish their own quilts. I read every book on the market (both of them) and talked to other professional quilters (if they would talk to me) and searched for other businesses with the same objective (and found none). So, I collaborated with my husband on a business model, and we got very busy implementing it. We made some mistakes, but we learned a lot and now would like to share our knowledge and help quilters transition confidently from rookie to expert.

Most quilters know how to sew, and so did I. But my sewing experience did not prepare me for the world of quilting. I remember the first time my good friend, Maria, tried to describe a rotary cutter to me. I could not imagine why a razor-blade weapon was necessary for quilting. Then she told me about free-motion quilting on a home machine. I wasn't sure what feed-dogs were, much less how to drop them.

After retiring, I did a special project as a computer consultant. Suddenly I had some spending money, and I remembered seeing a longarm quilting machine in our local quilt shop. I told my husband I wanted to buy a new sewing machine. Boy was he surprised! But he was so intrigued with its engineering, he hardly complained about losing his pool table and dart board to make room for it.

Once the machine was delivered and my initial fears were overcome, the idea of a retail quilting studio took form. I really thought I knew everything I needed to know to set up a small business. Wow, was I in for a shock. I had retired after over twenty years of experience in Information Systems with a major corporation. I assumed that if I could teach e-mail to sales people, I could teach quilters to use a longarm quilting machine. That was the last time my business assumptions were accurate.

This book is written for the benefit of any quilter who wants to start her (or his!) own longarm quilting business. It talks "About" the longarm quilting world and describes the "Basic" techniques for running the machine. And I describe the necessary steps toward building "Confidence" so you are ready to start your own business and take in customer quilts. I believe quilting is one of the most creative and satisfying occupations possible, and I am really encouraged by the incredible growth of the quilting industry.

I hope this book provides a path for you to travel so you can avoid many of the mistakes that I have made. I invite all of you to share your personal experiences with me, too. Please write to me in care of Krause Publications, Iola, WI. I would love to hear from you!

To Al, without your support this would still be a dream.

Contents

About
Longarm Quilting

This first section describes the terms and tools of longarm quilting. The concepts presented also apply to quilting on a short-arm machine or a domestic machine using a quilting frame. If you are using a machine that sits on a platform and can move in all directions across the quilt, this book is for you.

It is a good idea to read the entire section before you begin to quilt. It is also a good idea to come back and read it again after a little practice so the information can be understood more completely.

Having taught hundreds of quilting classes, I have found there are two types of quilters: artists and engineers. Therefore, many of the techniques and concepts presented in this book are described two ways: one way for the artist and one way for the engineer.

ARTISTS TEND TO BELIEVE:
- Pattern directions are merely suggestions
- There are no such things as "perfect points"
- Unscripted and spontaneous methods provide inspiration

ENGINEERS FIRMLY BELIEVE:
- Accuracy is everything
- Measuring and pre-planning lead to perfection
- Knowing exactly how the machine works is important

"Artists" and "Engineers" are terms of endearment and should not be taken personally. Most of us have characteristics of both.

The Machine

Artists: The machine head is similar to a domestic sewing machine except it is much larger and it is mounted on a platform that enables it to float across the surface of the quilt and move in any direction.

Engineers: The stitching mechanics are simple. The machine head pushes the needle into the fabric, taking the thread down into the bobbin area where a hook catches the thread and wraps it around the bobbin case to begin the stitch. A lever pulls on the top thread removing the slack and completing the stitch.

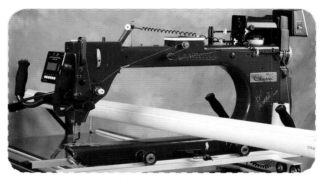

Longarm quilt machine

The Needle and Foot

Artists: The movement of the needle bar and hopping foot are precisely timed to work together as a unit.

Engineers: When the hopping foot descends, it compresses the fabric layers and holds them for a split second. In that split second, the needle enters the fabric, the hook grabs the thread and wraps it around the bobbin to form a stitch and comes back up.

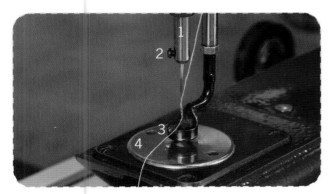

1. Needle bar 2. Needle set screw 3. Hopping foot
4. Needle base plate

The needle bar (1) and set screw (2) hold the needle and move it up and down with incredible precision. The needle base plate (4) is a metal plate with a hole in it that allows the needle to drop into the bobbin area. The hopping foot (3) is the sewing foot that surrounds the needle, and it really does hop! Most long-arm machines have circular hopping feet that measure ¼" from the tip of the needle to the outer edge of the foot.

The needle has a groove in the front which protects the thread and guides it toward the eye of the needle. It also has an indentation in the back, called the scarf, where the hook almost touches the needle. When inserting a new needle, be sure to push it up into the needle bar as far as it will go. Be careful not to twist the needle when tightening the set screw.

groove

The groove is in front

scarf

The scarf goes in back

Bobbin Assembly

The bobbin case holds the bobbin of thread, allowing the bobbin to rotate as the thread is drawn off during the stitching process. The hook catches the top thread and wraps it around the bobbin case.

The hook race spins around the bobbin case, and it catches the top thread when the needle descends. The hook comes within millimeters of the needle scarf (indentations in the back of the needle).

hook →

Thread from the bobbin is drawn through the bobbin case

The timing tool is a special spacer that helps align the position of the needle and the hook. If the needle and hook are not set properly, there will be skipped stitches.

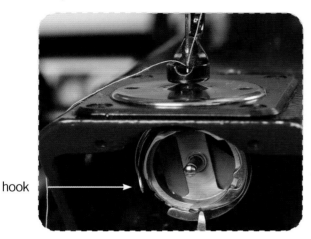

hook →

The hook catches the top thread

The timing tool ensures exact needle positioning

hint
When inserting the bobbin into the bobbin case, make sure the bobbin turns in the correct direction when the thread is pulled out. On most machines, the bobbin turns clockwise. Check the instructions that come with your machine to be sure.

Tension Devices

Adjusting the tension on the thread is a skill that every longarm quilter must master. The fabrics, battings, backings and threads are all variables which affect the stitch quality. Adjusting the thread tension is how the machine settings can be changed to accommodate these variables and produce a good stitch.

Takeup lever

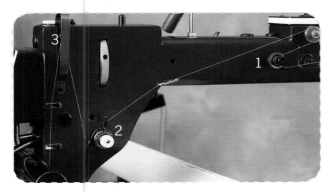

1. Intermittent tensioner 2. Rotary tensioner 3. Takeup lever

Intermittent tensioner

Rotary-tension device and check spring

(1) The intermittent tensioner adds tension to the top thread and ensures that the thread is drawn off the cone smoothly. (2) The rotary tension assembly feeds the thread to the takeup lever. It contains the check spring which helps the takeup lever remove the slack from the thread, making the stitch secure. (3) The takeup lever is attached to the needle bar, lets the thread be drawn down into the bobbin area and then pulls the thread back up. Stroke is the term for the up/down motion of the needle (and needle bar).

tip Place the cone of thread so it points straight up. Thread must be pulled straight up to avoid twisting the thread, which can cause breakage. If the cone is tilted, the thread pulls off unevenly, which can also cause breakage. Slippery threads (like monofilaments) need to be contained by a nylon mesh.

Enhanced Machine Functionality

Artists: A stitch regulator is a device that ensures the quilting stitches are all the same length. It has become very popular in recent years and many machines have them.

Engineers: Encoders (which are attached to the wheels) will sense how fast the machine head is moving, and in which direction. The information determines when the next stitch should be made. One encoder is clearly visible because it rides on one of the wheels on the machine head. The other is connected to the wheels on the crosstrack.

encoders

Stitch regulators need sensors called encoders

The needle positioner is a device that allows the needle to stop in the down position when the sewing head stops. This feature prevents the sewing head from moving accidentally.

The needle positioner switch controls single-stitch operation

If there is a horizontal channel lock, it will be attached to the machine head, and it will lock onto the crosstrack. This prevents the machine from moving back and forth, meaning it will only stitch side-to-side. The vertical channel lock is located on the crosstrack.

The horizontal channel lock is on the machine head

Some machines feature an on-board bobbin winder. It is usually attached to the side of the machine head. An on-board bobbin winder will wind the bobbins while you are quilting, using a separate cone of thread.

On-board bobbin winder

Machine-Head Gadgets

Most machine manufacturers will include some gadgets that make the quilting process easier. If they are not included, they can be purchased and are well worth the cost.

An extended base plate is an accessory that enlarges the base plate surface area, making it easier to use rulers and templates.

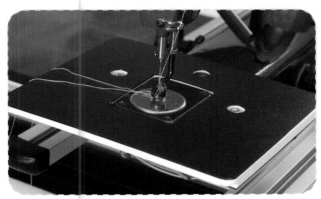

An extended base plate makes using rulers much easier

A laser light is similar to a tiny spot light that beams a small red light. It has a clamp that secures it to the machine head. It can be moved from the front to the back of the machine head, depending on the style of quilting.

A stylus is a pencil-like rod with a pointed end. The laser light is clamped to the stylus when doing pantographs. The stylus is also used to lock the machine onto a mechanical template to help stitch more accurate designs.

The stylus is used horizontally to hold the laser light

The stylus is used vertically when connecting to a mechanical template

Machine Maintenance

Each machine manufacturer has published procedures for maintaining their equipment. You should always perform the recommended maintenance procedures (at the recommended intervals) for your brand of machine.

Daily Maintenance

•Before you begin quilting, clean the machine head, removing any lint or oil that may have wicked onto the sewing area. Check the wheels and tracks for stray threads and lint.

•While quilting, brush out the lint from the bobbin case area every time the bobbin is changed. Add a single drop of oil to the bobbin area every other time the bobbin is changed.

•After quilting, clean the machine and perform the daily oiling. There are eight spots that get oiled on my machine. In addition to the seven shown here, there is one on the bobbin hook assembly.

> **tip** Vacuum the tracks (or rails) on the crosstrack and table to prevent dust build-up.

1. Oil reservoir near the motor

2. On the side

3. On the bobbin winder post

4 & 5. Two oil ports covered with little silver spheres that push down

6 & 7. Two oil ports are white plastic surrounding the wicks

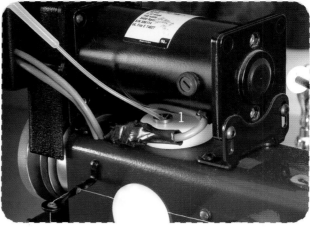
Oiling location in the back

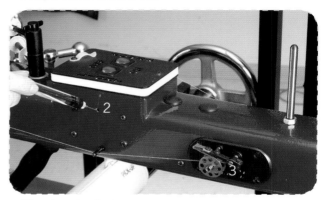
Oiling location in the middle

Two of the spots are covered with a small sphere. Push it down to get the oil in. The other two have the wick visible

Tool-Kit Items

The tools you need to do routine mainte-nance should come with your machine. In ad-dition to these tools, there are some household items that are useful:

1. Paintbrush for removing lint (no larger than one inch)
2. Hex wrenches in multiple sizes
3. Cotton-tip swabs
4. Timing tool
5. Screw drivers, small and medium in both flat and Phillips head
• Flashlight (I prefer a Snake Light) — not shown
• Long-handle tweezers - not shown

tip I highly recommend a tool kit to keep all the tools and spare parts together in a convenient spot. Hide it in your studio so no other family members will be tempted to "borrow" your tools.

Always have extra spare parts on hand:
• Check spring
• Fuse
• "O" rings
• Switches

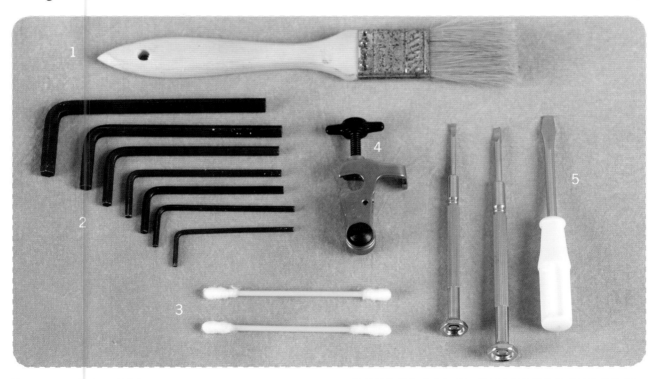

Recommended tool-kit items

tip Take digital photos during any maintenance procedures and keep a maintenance log for future reference.

Crosstrack

The crosstrack (or carriage) is a platform that supports and guides the machine head. It is designed to allow the machine head to move freely in any direction. The table is essentially a giant quilt frame that holds the fabric in place.

Artists: The crosstrack holds the machine head.

Engineers: The machine has wheels that sit on the rails of the crosstrack. These wheels enable the machine to roll from front-to-back. The crosstrack also has its own wheels that fit in the rails on the table. These wheels enable the machine to move from side-to-side.

If your machine has a vertical channel lock, it will be on the crosstrack. The locking mechanism is magnetic, and it locks the crosstrack carriage onto the metal table frame. When the track is locked onto the table, the machine can't move horizontally, resulting in perfectly straight vertical lines.

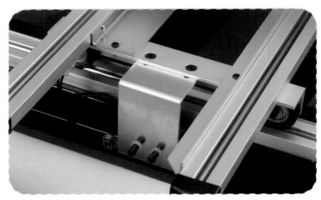

The vertical channel lock is on the crosstrack

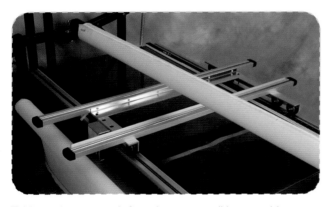

Table and crosstrack for a longarm quilting machine

Table

Artists: The primary purpose of the table is to hold the layers of the quilt securely in place so you can stitch them together without wrestling.

Engineers: The table top is a long, flat surface that is usually covered by a clear plastic sheet. Rolled paper patterns (for stitching edge-to-edge designs) fit on the table top, under the clear plastic. When using these patterns, the quilter is working from the back of the machine using a stylus or laser light to trace the designs.

Leaders

Attached to three of the rollers are pieces of canvas called leaders. The quilt is attached to the leaders with pins or zippers.

Clamps

Clamps (or side clamps) are used to gently stretch the fabric sideways. The clamp attaches to the backing and is secured snugly to the table sides, providing extra tension and reducing any sagging.

The table top (shown from the back) holds patterns in place

Clamps secure the quilt on the sides

Rollers

Artists: The rollers work together to perform the "stretcher" functions.

Engineers: Tension is controlled by rotating the rollers with the hand wheel and holding them in place using the locking lever. The rollers have a gear-like collar on one end, and the locking lever fits into one of the cogs at the end of the roller.

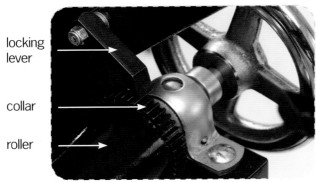

locking lever

collar

roller

Locking lever maintains tension on the rollers

The pick-up roller (or takeup roller) has a leader that attaches to the top edge of the quilt backing. Finished portions of the quilt get wrapped on this roller as it is advanced. The height can be adjusted to maintain a level quilting surface.

The backing roller (or lining roller) has a leader that attaches to the bottom edge of the quilt back.

The top roller (or quilt-top roller) has a leader that attaches to the bottom edge of the quilt top.

The belly bar (or carrier roller) is just about belly height. It holds the quilt in place, like one edge of a big quilt frame. The opposite edge is being held by the pick-up roller, and the sides are held by the side clamps.

The stabilizer bar lifts and separates the batting and backing.

The batting bar is a metal pole under the table top where batting is stored.

hand adjustment crank

hand wheel

The pick-up roller can be raised using the height adjustment crank

A pivotal access assembly can be flipped up to expose the quilt layers and smooth the batting if needed. It has two positions for normal quilting. Load position facilitates easy loading and quilt position allows the quilter to sit if they choose.

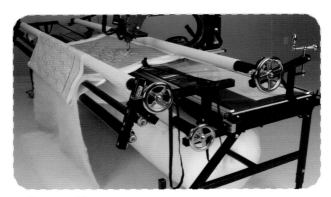

Open position

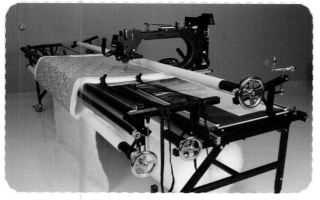

Load position

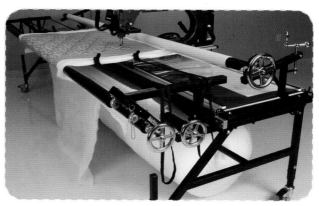

Quilt position

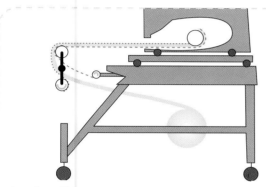

Load position

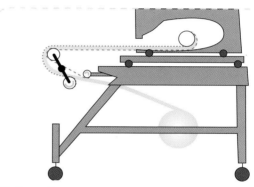

Quilt position

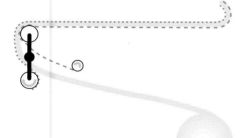

Load position detail

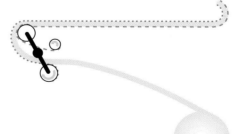

Quilt position detail

tip Take a photo or draw a diagram of the proper loading path for your table because it is easy to forget when first starting out!

Optional Table Accessories

Each machine manufacturer offers different equipment options. The value of these options will vary depending on the type of quilting you do.

Light Bar

Some tables have a frame that holds a line of light fixtures which illuminate the entire quilting surface from above.

The light bar provides direct lighting

Quilting Chair

It is possible to sit while quilting by using a chair on rollers. Quilting chairs have casters which fit over a rail on a mat that lays on the floor in front of the machine. The rail guides the chair side-to-side while keeping it parallel to the belly bar for improved control.

A chair on rollers fits onto the track

Fabric Advance

Some tables have an automatic fabric advancing feature. At the push of a button (or pedal), all layers advance simultaneously.

Table Height Adjustments

Some tables have a hydraulic lift to raise and lower the table height. Proper table height helps maintain good posture and personal comfort.

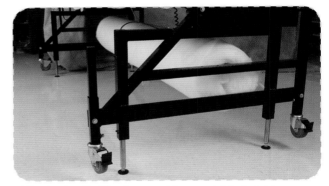

The hydraulic lift raises and lowers table height

Zipper Leaders

When zippers are attached to the canvas leaders, the quilt can be removed from the table and reloaded without the layers shifting.

Zipper leaders make reloading a quilt possible and perfect

Basic Operation

These pages are devoted to getting the machine ready to sew. Simplified instructions for turning on the power, threading the machine, loading the bobbin and starting to stitch are given here. Refer to your owner's manual for details on your brand of machine.

Power Up

The power and light switches are usually located on the top of the sewing head, about in the middle so they can be reached from both the front and back of the machine. Sometimes there is a light fixture just above the needle area that will have a separate switch. Laser lights usually have separate power switches, too.

The power switch needs to be turned on

The laser light switch

Threading the Machine

The instructions here describe how to thread the machine shown in the photos. Check your user manual for the exact instructions for your machine.

Step 1 Start in the back of the machine, and follow the path shown in the first photo. Be sure the thread fits between the tension disks on the intermittent tensioner.

The thread path runs from the cone through the guides, through the intermittent tensioner to the break sensor

Step 2 Move to the front of the machine and continue the threading as shown in the second photo. Be sure the thread catches the check spring on the second wrap around the rotary tensioner.

From the break sensor, the thread runs through the guides, rotary tensioner and check spring to the takeup lever

Step 3 Finish by threading the needle. Be sure it is threaded from front to back.

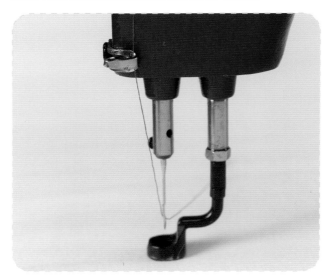

The thread goes through the guides and is threaded from front to back through the eye of the needle

tip Each machine manufacturer should have a technical manual (as well as a user manual) for their machines. If you don't have one, consult their website or call directly to get the mechanical information you need. It is always best to start by following the manufacturer's recommendations, but keep your mind open to suggestions made by others. Sometimes a homemade remedy is just great!

Loading the Bobbin

The steps here should work for most machines, but check your user manual for the exact instructions for your machine.

Step 1 Place the bobbin into the case, leaving a tail of thread pulled out. Guide the thread tail into the slot in the bobbin case and under the tension bar as shown.

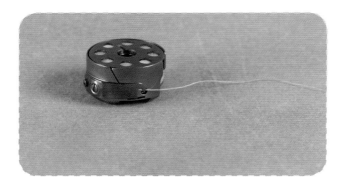

Thread the bobbin case

Step 2 Put the bobbin case into the machine, aligning the notch as shown. You should hear a distinct click.

bobbin case handle   alignment notch

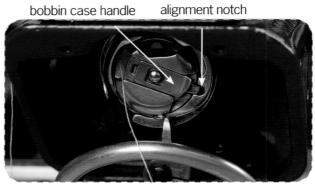

Insert the bobbin case

tip Be sure the bobbin thread does not get caught under the bobbin case handle. If it does, the bobbin thread tension is too tight and stitch quality is poor.

Machine Supplies

tip Any replacement part that is directly involved in the quality of stitches should be purchased from the manufacturer or dealer.

Bobbins

Bobbins are an integral part of the rotary-hook assembly, so order them from your machine dealer. The bobbins for most longarm machines are size M. They hold at least two times as much thread as a standard bobbin used in a domestic sewing machine. Bobbins can be filled using the bobbin winder on your machine (most have them now) or using a stand-alone bobbin winder. Pre-wound bobbins are also now available in size M.

Size M bobbins hold much more thread than standard bobbins

Bobbin Case

A bobbin case is an integral part of the rotary hook assembly, so only buy extras from your machine dealer. The bobbin case has an anti-backlash spring (blue back plate) on the inside to prevent the bobbin from spinning after the machine head has stopped. Springs should be purchased from your machine dealer.

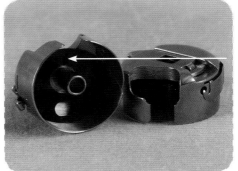

blue back plate

Bobbin cases have anti-backlash springs

tip I highly recommend keeping an extra bobbin case. Some threads work better on top if you use them with very fine, almost invisible thread in the bobbin. These fine threads require a different bobbin-case tension setting. Rather than changing the tension frequently, I recommend you keep one bobbin case for standard threads, and have one for fine threads.

Bobbin Winder

The external bobbin winder is an alternative to the on-board bobbin winder. It has its own tension disks that help ensure a tight and evenly wound bobbin.

The thread should be pulled straight up off the cone, through the thread guide and around the tension disks. Wrap the thread around the center of an empty bobbin, or guide the thread through the hole in the side of the bobbin (if any). Push the lever that controls the amount of thread that gets wound onto the bobbin. An arm should move into place over the bobbin. When the bobbin is almost full and the thread level reaches that arm, the lever pops up, and the winding stops automatically. Remember to keep an even pressure on the foot pedal as it winds.

Oil

The oil used in most longarm machines is special. It is designed to dissipate, which

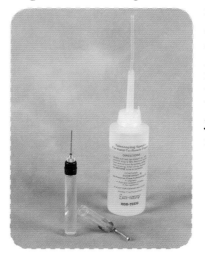

means if you get oil on your quilt top, it will disappear in 24-48 hours. Any oil that has turned yellow is not safe for your quilts.

Oil dispensers help deliver the right amount of oil

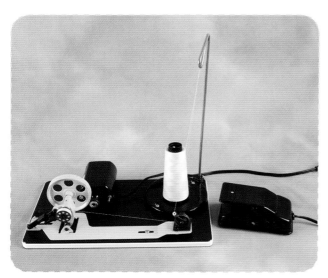

External bobbin winder

Quilting Supplies

These supplies are designed just for quilters, regardless of the size or type of machine they use. You will soon discover that certain supplies work very well with your machine, and others don't. Initially, ask your dealer for brands that are known to work well with your machine. Later, when you need to replenish your supplies, try some of the new items on the market.

Patterns

For hand-guided machines, the patterns are usually paper, and a laser light is used to follow the pattern. The designs are frequently made up of one continuous line, which, when repeated across the quilt, span the area from edge-to-edge. Pantograph is a term that describes this process.

Paper patterns are traced using a laser light or stylus

Tape Measures

Tape measures are a necessary tool for your quilting studio, and fortunately, there are new styles that will make your life much easier. Centering tape measures are great when loading a quilt and when advancing the quilt. Sticky-back tape measures really help when planning and stitching cross-hatching designs.

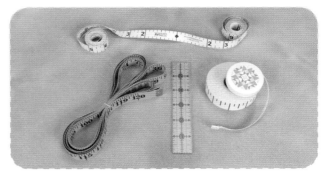

Tape measures come in many designs

Stencils

Stencils are guides for marking designs directly on the quilt top. Most sewers are familiar with stencils made for hand quilters. Machine quilters can use these same stencils if they can determine how to stitch the design in one continuous line of stitching.

Stencils are used to mark designs for free-motion quilting

Templates

Near-perfect stitch lines are possible by running the machine's foot along the edge of the template. Templates can be long or short, straight or curved.

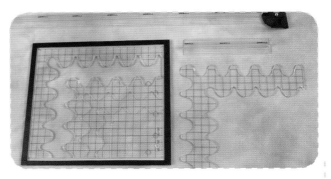

Templates guide the machine to make perfect stitch lines and curves

Crochet hook

When I discover my stray thread clippings have worked their way into the quilt layers, I use a tiny crochet hook to carefully separate the fabric threads and hook the stray clipping so I can extract it. This is really tough to do if you have already quilted over the area, but sometimes you don't see the stray threads until you stitch over them.

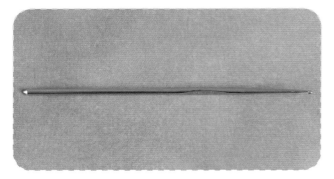

Try a crochet hook to remove stray threads

Retractable Scissors Holder

This is like putting your scissors on a leash and attaching the leash to your clothing. It sounds dorky, but your friends will eventually understand that you consider your retractable-scissors holder (and attached scissors) to be the latest in fashionable jewelry for the long-arm quilter!

A retractable scissors holder attaches to clothing

Tweezers

Tweezers are used to grab threads from tight spaces and to remove linty gunk from the table, machine or bobbin area. Long, skinny ends are desirable.

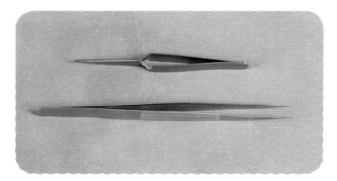

Tweezers are used to remove threads that fingers can't reach

Quilt-Layer Choices

The quilt top may be "center stage," but the batting, backing and thread help "spotlight" the quilt top. The choices made for a quilt help define its character.

Batting

There are many choices in batting. Some of the variables are loft, content, care and price. Here are some hints to consider before making a choice or recommendation.

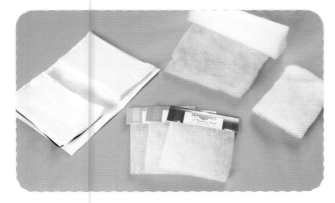

Commercial batting products

•Bed quilts are generally not quilted very densely, unless they are a show piece only. Wall hangings can be very densely quilted, especially when the quilting stitches provide some of the details of the piece. Low-loft battings are usually more appropriate for wall hangings.

Low-loft, compressed batting for a flat wall hanging

•When quilting stitches are used to add background detail, the batting can help accentuate the detail.

Medium-loft, fluffy batting adds some detail

•When batting is used to add dimension and draw attention to a focal point, high-loft batting is used. Trapunto is a good example.

High-loft, fluffy batting provides bold accents

•Very traditional quilt tops may look better with a thinner, natural-fiber batting that drapes nicely.

•If shrinkage is not desirable, be sure to pre-shrink the batting or choose one with minimal shrinkage (one percent shrinkage is good). Many polyester battings claim 0-1% shrinkage; natural fibers tend to shrink more and may need extra care when washing.

•When selecting a batting for a quilt that will be washed regularly, it is probably wise to avoid any batting that can't be put into the dryer, or that needs to be blocked.

•Evaluations of battings seem to agree that low-loft, cotton batting does tend to wrinkle more. A fold line from shipping or storage might be harder to remove from cotton than from other fiber contents, and the quilt may not hang flat.

tip
If you must fold your quilts for any length of time, do it in thirds to avoid any creases in the center.

Selecting the Backing

tip For economic reasons, most quilters have been tempted to use inexpensive materials on the back. Remember that the backing is just as visible as the top so choose a good quality fabric that will wear well.

Light color backing showcases stitching

• Choose a busy print if you want the stitches to be disguised. When I do heavy outline quilting with multiple thread colors, I generally use the same color bobbin thread, and I adjust the tension to pull more toward the back to ensure the bobbin thread stays on the back. As a result, sometimes I can see pin dots of thread from the front coming through to the back, which a busy printed backing can help disguise.

Dense stitching adds definition; busy prints help hide quilting stitch irregularities

• Choose a solid, light or neutral color if you want the stitches to "pop," showcasing the quilting stitches. But beware, with this technique, tension problems will also be showcased.

• Choose a fabric that has similar fiber content and characteristics as your quilt top. Avoid bedsheets that have a high thread count if possible. Similarly, avoid batik fabrics until you know how your machine will handle stiffer fabrics.

• If you have pre-washed the fabrics in the quilt top, then pre-wash the backing, too. Press the backing after washing if it is wrinkled.

• When you need to sew multiple pieces together to get the necessary size, be sure to trim off all selvage edges. If this is not possible, snip small perpendicular cuts into the selvage to reduce any warp from the shrinkage.

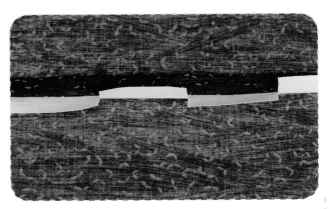

Cut small slits in the selvage edge to minimize shrinkage

Selecting the Thread

Machine quilting threads come in a wonderful variety of colors, content and sizes. The tension on the longarm machine might need to be tweaked to accommodate some specialty threads. If you aren't comfortable with adjusting tension yet, try to stay with a brand of thread that works well with your machine.

Audition thread colors by laying the thread on the quilt top

If possible, use the same color in the top and the bobbin. Any time different colors are used, there is a risk that the color from one side will show up on the opposite side. With busy prints this is not a problem. With solid-color fabrics and high-contrast thread colors, you will be able to see pin dots of color.

Variegated threads change color. They may disappear into the fabric if the prints are busy or the thread color matches the fabric. Variegated threads really stand out on solid fabrics. Landscape quilts frequently use variegated threads to achieve special effects.

Variegated thread adds character

tip Technically, "color blocked" means changing colors, and variegated means changing shades of the same color. But, the word "variegated" is frequently used to describe either variation.

Threads are now available in a multitude of materials. The most common threads for quilting are cotton and cotton-wrapped poly. Recent improvements in the industry enable us to use thread made of polyester, monofilament, rayon, metal and even starch.

Almost any thread can be used in art quilts

Cotton thread comes in many colors and weights but is not as strong as some of the other quilting threads on the market.

Cotton-wrapped poly is exactly what it sounds like. Cotton fibers are wrapped around a polyester core, providing extra strength, making it easier to use than 100% cotton.

Thread content is difficult to determine without the label

Metallic thread is fussy but beautiful

Polyester and poly wrapped poly are also stronger than cotton. Recent improvements in machine quilting threads have provided us with a thread that looks and acts like cotton but is more durable. What a match!

Monofilament is an (almost) invisible filament that works well for outline quilting. It actually comes in two colors: clear and smoke. The smoke has a gray tint to it that serves to minimize light reflection – it's a good choice for dark fabrics. Use the clear monofilament on light fabrics.

Monofilament is called "invisible" but it comes in two colors

Metallic threads can be fussy. Most metallic threads are flat instead of round. (Using a needle intended for metallic threads is a good idea). The metal heats up due to friction, and hot metallic thread breaks much faster than cool thread, which means it breaks more. So skip some of the thread guides, and stitch slowly. If needed, adjust the tension, allowing the top metallic thread to almost lay flat, and have the bobbin thread doing all the work. Use a really thin filament thread in the bobbin, so it doesn't take away from the visual effect of the metallic thread.

Water-soluble threads are made from starch. Trapunto is a technique that depends on the water-soluble thread to be strong enough to hold the first layer of batting in place while the excess is trimmed away (and this can take days) and still dissolve in water without excessive agitation.

tip Serger thread is not recommended for quilting because it is not strong enough to endure typical quilt usage. Lightweight threads will break when someone sits on a quilt stitched with them. Art quilts rarely need to endure weight bearing, so if strength isn't an issue, serger thread is just fine.

tip Thread choices for quilting are made in conjunction with other elements. Thread breakage can be an issue if the quilt top has been constructed with multiple layers of fusible webbing. Additional factors that affect thread breakage include the type of fusible webbing, number of layers, content of fabrics, etc. Naturally the needle size, table tension and quilting speed are factors, too.

Selecting the Needles

I am a believer in using the same needles that the machine manufacturer or dealer recommends. My favorite size is 3.5 but I own four different sizes: MR 3.0, MR 3.5, MR 4.0, and MR 5.0. The larger the number, the thicker the needle. Because the machines are timed to have the hook almost touch the needle, the thickness of the needle is a timing factor. My machine is timed using a MR 3.5 needle, so I can use a 3.0 or 4.0 without worry. If I use the largest MR 5.0 needle, I probably will need to re-time my longarm machine.

Change the needle every quilt or two. Polyester batting seems to dull needles faster than cotton or wool. Regardless of how long I have used a needle, when I hear a popping sound, I change it. Needles that are dull or have a burr can actually push the batting out so it is visible on the back.

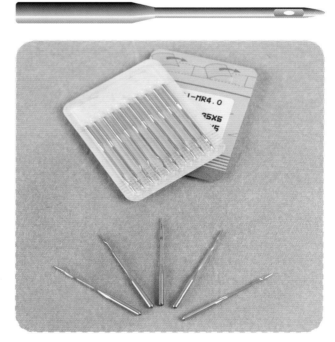

Use the brand of needle recommended for your machine

Winding Bobbins

If you are winding a bobbin for the first time and you plan to use the on-board bobbin winder, you will be running your longarm at constant speed without sewing, so unthread the needle and remove the bobbin case.

tip The thread must stay securely inside the tension disks during the entire bobbin winding process. If the tension is too loose or the thread pops out, the thread will continue to wind, but it will be loose and have a spongy feel. Adjust the tension by rotating the knob on the tension assembly; right to tighten, left to loosen. If the thread won't stay between the tension disks, it is probably too tight.

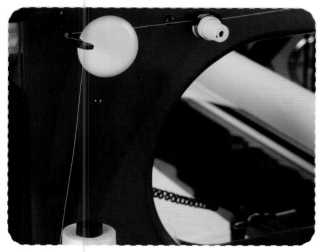

Feed thread through guides and tension assembly

Position the empty bobbin, secure the thread and position the bar

Step 1 Put the cone of thread on the machine.

Step 2 Feed the thread up through the guide above the cone and through the guides that lead to the tension assembly.

Step 3 Wrap the thread around the tension disk once being sure the thread goes between the tension disks.

Step 4 Put an empty bobbin on the spindle and turn it until it clicks into place.

Step 5 Feed the thread through the guides up to the bobbin.

Step 6 Wrap the thread around the bobbin a few times, securing the end.

Step 7 Lower the bar into the center of the bobbin. This bar stops the winding mechanism when the bobbin is full. Be sure it is positioned properly.

Step 8 Put the machine into manual mode (not stitch regulated), and turn the machine on. The bobbin should be winding.

At this time, if you need that bobbin before you can quilt anything, you must run the machine at a constant speed and wait until the bobbin is full. If this is a spare bobbin, you can resume your quilting, and the spare bobbin will be wound while you sew. (Don't forget to put the machine back into stitch-regulated mode and re-thread the needle). When the bobbin is full, it will stop winding automatically.

Check the tension on the bobbin case by putting a full bobbin into the case and threading it. Lift the case by the thread tail. The case should turn on its side, but you should not be able to lift it off the table.

To adjust the tension, find two tiny screws that hold down the bobbin-tension bar. The larger one sets the tension, and the smaller one holds the tension bar in place. Both are very easy to strip and/or drop, so be very careful. Only turn the screw about one hour at a time. In other words, turn it $1/12$ of a turn – or 30 degrees – at a time.

tip Check that the backlash spring is in place. This spring keeps the bobbin from spinning when you stop sewing. Check that the thread on the bobbin is wound on securely; it should not be spongy.

Stitch Regulator

The next few paragraphs are devoted to the Gammill Plus stitch regulator and other stitch settings. For people who own other machines, the concepts will be similar, but the buttons may be different.

Gammill Plus control panel and screen

There are two sensor lights above the screen. The red light goes on when there is an alert message showing on the screen. Alert messages happen when the machine senses that the thread has broken or that the bobbin thread is low. The green light goes on when the machine is on and the stitch regulator is enabled.

There are six buttons below the screen:

•"H" and "V" are the horizontal- and vertical-channel locks. When you press the button, the light turns on, and a magnet engages, which locks the machine head into a fixed position. If you press "H," your lines of stitching will be parallel to the rollers; "V" means the stitching will be perpendicular to the rollers. Press the buttons again to disengage the magnets. Press them both, and the machine head will lock in place, which is very handy when cleaning the lint or threading the needle.

•"A" stands for automatic mode. If the screen says "Regulated ...", you are in automatic mode and the stitch regulator is on.

•"M" is for manual mode. If the screen says "Motor Speed x%", you are in manual mode and the stitch regulator is off.

•"+" and "-" buttons are used to change certain settings. In regulated mode, the +/- buttons control the stitches per inch. In manual mode, the +/- buttons control the motor speed.

Needle-positioner switch

To run the machine in regulated mode:

• Move the machine to your quilt.

• Press the left button to take a single stitch.

• Pull up the bobbin thread.

• Press the right button. The machine beeps and it is ready to stitch.

• Move the machine to begin stitching. Press the right button again to stop stitching.

If you have a needle positioner, look at the toggle switch on the left side of the screen. Single Stitch means pressing the left (black) button will initiate a full single stitch. Needle Position means pressing the left button will initiate a half stitch. If the needle is in the down position when you press the red button to start, it will go back to the down position when you press the red button again to stop. Very handy!

The two buttons in the handles control the stitching. The red button in the right handle is the Start/Stop button. When you press this button, the green enabled light turns on, there is a brief pause and a short beep. Be sure to wait for the beep before moving the machine. The black button in the left handle is the Single-Stitch/Needle-Position button. When you press this, you take one single stitch, or one half stitch, depending on the needle positioner setting.

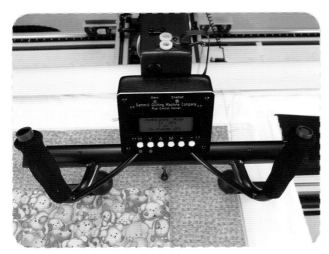

Handle buttons control stitching

Quilting the Quilt

The quilting process generally includes four phases: stabilizing, stitching the motifs, borders and backgrounds. Not all designs need all phases and the phases aren't always done in this sequence.

Phase 1: Stabilizing the Quilt

The purpose of stabilizing is to control distortion. Each stitch compresses the backing, batting and top. The denser the quilting, the more distortion there will be. If dense quilting only happens in parts of the quilt, the rest of the quilt will puff up and wrinkle.

Stitch-in-the-ditch is a regular-length stitch that is used to stabilize an area of a quilt and is not removed. Below, I've listed several situations where stabilizing is necessary.

Stabilizing Blocks to Contain Distortion

Individual blocks that will have a quilted motif and some background filler need to be stabilized to contain distortion. When stabilizing individual blocks, start with the blocks in the center and work out to the sides.

Stabilizing Border Seams

Like a picture frame, the border frames the body of the quilt. By stabilizing the border seams before quilting the center, the quilt maintains its shape and resists the hourglass effect. This is especially useful when the side borders are done last. Use a centering tape measure to keep accurate measurements.

Stabilizing the Outer Edges

The top edge is basted as part of the quilt-loading process. The side edges are basted a section at a time, and the bottom edge is basted last. Once the bottom edge has been basted, remove the leader attached to the quilt top. If you don't, you won't be able to roll the quilt back up to work on the upper sections again.

Phase 2: Stitching the Motifs

After the quilt is stabilized, the continuous line motifs are stitched. By definition, a continuous-line design has only one start and one stop and sometimes these are the same spot. Pantograph is a common name for a continuous line design that can be stitched from one edge of a quilt to the other. They usually fill the space well enough that there is no need for additional background stitching.

Phase 3: Borders

Like the motifs, borders are usually continuous-line designs. The complexity of the design chosen for the borders will determine the stitching sequence.

Usually the corners are done first, and then the border is stitched in one continuous line, connecting the corners. The top and bottom borders are done first. When the top, bottom and body of the quilt are done, the quilt is removed from the table and turned. The side borders (which are now positioned at the top and bottom) are stitched in one continuous line, connecting the corners that were done earlier. Variations in the measurements are easier to manage when the entire border is visible.

Phase 4: Backgrounds

Background quilting is usually denser than the motif quilting, compressing the background so the motif puffs up.

Background fillers are usually done last because they are most likely to distort the fabric. The filler design is chosen to complement the quilt. They may be very subtle like stippling, or fillers may be a bit more distinctive like radiating lines. A very popular style of filler is called McTavishing which reads like a textured background. The style of quilt will be a factor in selecting a complementary filler style.

Basic Skills

This section of the book describes basic skills and common techniques used in longarm quilting. These techniques have evolved over time and are now the foundation for some beautiful quilting styles. Practicing these techniques will improve your control of the machine.

Prepare the Quilt

Check the Quilt Top

The first step in preparing a quilt is to check the construction, looking for problem areas. Check to see if the measurements are the same at both edges and in the middle. If they are different, you can sometimes ease in extra fullness with framing strips.

> **tip** An easy way to compare the dimensions of a quilt is to fold the sides of the quilt in, meeting at the middle. You can instantly see if the outer edges differ in length from the center and by how much.

Press the Quilt Top

Pressing the quilt top and backing enables you to check for problems in the seam allowances like thread knots and separating seams. The outer edges of a quilt top shouldn't have bias edges but if they are there, be very careful not to stretch them.

Trim the Quilt Top

Trimming the threads from the quilt top helps prevent shadowing. Be sure to cut the threads; pulling threads out can cause seams to come undone.

Remove Embellishments

Embellishments enhance the look of the quilt top but are very difficult to quilt over or around. Hitting obstacles can also cause machine problems.

> **tip** Don't use fussy fabrics until after you and your machine have bonded. Fabrics that are stretchy make the quilt difficult to position and they pucker easily. Fabrics that are stiff make the stitch quality suffer. Both are possible to quilt but can be tricky, so get to know your machine before trying these.

Frame the Quilt Top

Framing means adding an extra strip of fabric to the outer edges of the quilt top, similar to adding another border around the quilt. The result is a more stable quilt top which makes the quilting process easier. Not all quilt tops need to be framed but beginners will benefit from the improved control. (See Basic Skill on page 41.)

Cut the Batting

If you are cutting batting from a roll, be sure to add three to four extra inches on all sides, just like the backing. After you are done quilting, the excess will be trimmed away. The batting needs to be as large as the quilt backing and free of any debris and wrinkles.

Fluff the batting to return it to its original shape and size. If using batting cut from a roll, you probably don't need to fluff it. Just be aware that the folds are the most likely places to have a wrinkle.

tip To fluff packaged batting, put it in a clothes dryer for a few minutes. The dryer will help release the wrinkles caused by the packaging. Be sure to keep the dryer on low especially with polyester batting.

Check the Backing Fabric

Be sure you have enough fabric for the backing. If necessary, the backing can be framed. Also, take a close look at the type of fabric. Backing fabric that has a significantly different weight or stretch than the quilt top can be problematic.

Measure the Backing

Make sure the backing is larger than the entire top (quilt top plus framing strips) by several inches in every direction. In other words, you will need a total of six to eight inches extra in length and in width.

Extra backing fabric on the side edges accommodates the clamps, keeping them far away from the quilting area to avoid stitching in distortion.

Extra fabric for clamps at the side

Extra backing fabric is required at the top and bottom to accommodate what is lost when the fabric is attached to the leaders (called the bite) and any differences in stretch. Extra length also allows the quilting stitches to extend past the bottom edge, when a pantograph pattern doesn't fit exactly.

Square Up the Backing

The backing must be squared up before it is loaded or it can sag. Backing fabric that sags will probably get tucks stitched into it.

One method of squaring the backing fabric is to tear it cross-grain. Another method is to trim the fabric so the measurements (length and width) are the same and the corners are square. Remove all selvage edges if possible.

tip   If you can't avoid having selvage edges in the backing area, cut a small slit perpendicular to the selvage edge half the distance from the edge to the seam. Slits will help relieve some of the tightness.

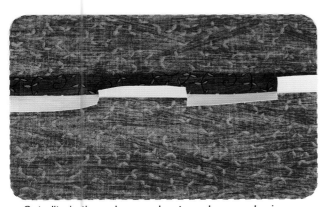

Cut slits in the selvage edge to reduce puckering

Framing

Framing means stitching a strip of extra fabric around the perimeter of the quilt. The advantages of framing are as follows:

•Stabilizes the sides of the quilt so the quilting can extend out to the very edge without puckering the fabric.
•Secures the border seams at the outer edges so they don't separate.
•Eases in any fullness in the quilt top to ensure the opposite sides are exactly the same size.
•Allows you to quilt off the edge when doing a pantograph that doesn't fit the quilt perfectly.
•Allows you to quilt off the edge when doing alternating motifs.

To frame a quilt, you will need:
•Muslin (or other cotton fabric) cut lengthwise (with the grain) into framing strips 3"-4" wide. Stitch the pieces together to make them long enough for the perimeter of the quilt.
•Domestic sewing machine with a straight stitch and other basic sewing supplies.

How to frame a quilt:

Step 1 Measure the length of the quilt top as you would if applying borders.

Step 2 Cut two pieces of the framing strip to fit.

Step 3 Pin the strips in place, easing in any fullness just as you would for a border.

Step 4 Stitch the strip onto the quilt top using a scant ¼" seam allowance.

Step 5 Repeat steps 1-4 (measure/cut/pin/stitch) for the width of the quilt, being sure to add the width of the framing strips.

tip When attaching framing strips use a scant ¼" seam allowance so there is no need to remove the muslin. The excess fabric is trimmed off after quilting and the stitch line is hidden inside the binding.

Use a scant ¼" when stay stitching

Sometimes it isn't possible or desirable to frame a quilt. If you don't frame the quilt, be sure to reinforce the seams by running a line of stitching around the outer edge a scant ¼" from the cut edge of the quilt top. This is called stay-stitching and is done on a domestic machine using a standard stitch length. When quilting an unframed quilt, be sure to baste all three layers together at each side to prevent the top from shifting. Keeping the basting line very close to the raw edge will keep the seam allowance from being caught by the hopping foot.

Loading the Quilt

This section describes how to load a quilt in general terms. Keep in mind that every machine is different so the techniques will vary slightly depending on your machine brand. One step in loading the quilt is pinning on. Learning to pin on is a basic skill for everyone regardless of your machine brand.

Pinning On

Pinning on (or stitching on) means attaching the quilt layers to the table by securing them to the canvas leaders. Most people use hat pins or T-pins to pin on. People with zipper leaders may prefer to sew the quilt top and/or backing to the detachable part of the zipper leader. Either way, you will need to master this basic skill.

General information:
•Use safety pins to mark the center points of all four sides of the backing. The center points at the top and bottom are used to position the fabric properly on the canvas leaders. The center points at the sides are used to monitor the stretch or shrinkage of the quilt top during quilting.

•The canvas leader should have the center point marked with a permanent marker (if the center is not marked, you will want to carefully measure and mark it). Place right and left edge reference pins in the canvas leader to help prevent stretched fabric when pinning on. Use the width of the fabric to determine where each edge pin should be. Example, if the fabric is 60" wide, one reference pin would be 30" to the right of center, and one would be 30" to the left of center.

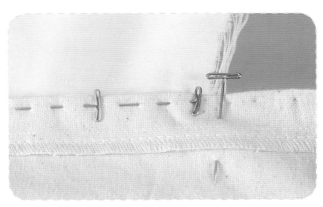

A reference pin marks the side edges

Safety pins mark the center points of all sides

•When pinning, the head of the pin should always be on the canvas side. Insert the pin into the canvas side first, about ¼" from the edge. (The ¼" space results in a ½" loss of fabric, called the bite.) Push the pin down through the canvas and fabric and back up, keeping the pin parallel with the edge of the leader. Keep pins evenly spaced, about ½" apart. Long pins can pierce the layers several times which helps distribute the stress. To prevent getting stuck, bury the tip of the pin inside the leader fabric.

How to pin on

Step 1 Align the center of the fabric to the center of the leader.

Step 2 Position the raw edge of the fabric even with the edge of the leader.

Step 3 Begin pinning (or stitching) at the center and work out to the reference pins at the edges. By pinning from the center to the side, the fabric will stay centered.

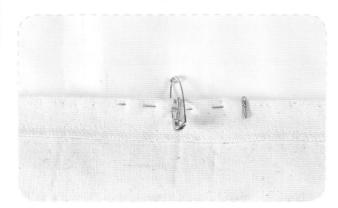

A pin marks the fabric center

Pinning On (continued)

tip Instead of pinning, it is possible to sew the fabric to the canvas if zipper leaders are being used. Use a large, long zig-zag stitch on a domestic machine. Align the center points, paying attention to how the zipper will zip onto the table. Most zipper leaders start at the right and pull to the left. Begin stitching at the center of the leader and work to one edge. Return to the center and stitch the other side. Repeat for all three leaders. Now just zip on.

Sewing the fabric to the zipper leaders eliminates pin pricks

Loading the Backing

Step 1 Position the backing fabric right side down over the rollers.

Step 2 Align the center points of fabric and canvas leader.

Step 3 Pin the top edge of the backing to the leader on the pick-up roller.

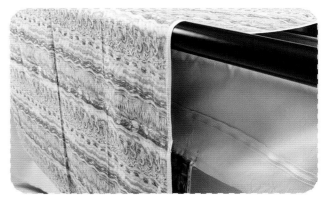

Check that the fabric is positioned properly

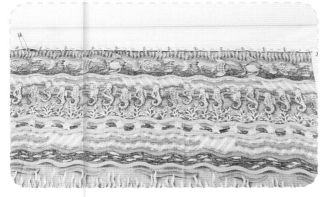

Be sure the backing fabric is right-side down

tip When attaching the backing to the leader, make sure the fabric is right side down. If the backing fabric is directional, make sure it is facing the right direction. If using zippers, be sure they are positioned properly.

Step 5 Tighten the backing. First, position the upper canvas edge to be somewhere in the middle of the quilting surface. This edge will be the guide when positioning the batting and securing the quilt top. Excess fabric is wound onto the lining roller on the bottom. Don't allow the fabric to wrinkle or it will pull unevenly. Use the locking levers to hold the roller in place.

Position the upper canvas edge within reach and tighten

Step 4 Align the centers and attach the bottom edge of the backing to the lining/backing roller. This process is the same as attaching the backing to the top edge. The biggest challenge here is to be sure the fabric is fed over and around the rollers properly. Refer to your manual if needed.

Loading the Quilt Top

A common method of loading the quilt top is called a partial float and that is what is described here. The upper edge of the quilt floats free, and the lower edge of the quilt is attached to a leader. (Another alternative, the full float, means the quilt top is not attached to any leader; it floats free.)

Step 1 Use safety pins to mark the center points of all four sides of the quilt top.

Step 2 Position the quilt top right side up over the rollers.

Step 3 Align the center points and pin the lower edge of the quilt top (or framing strip) to the leader of the front roller.

Roll the excess fabric onto the front roller

Step 5 Wind the top fabric onto the roller until the top edge of the quilt top meets the top edge of the backing. Flip the rest of the quilt top forward so the batting can be put in place.

Only the lower edge of the quilt top is attached to a leader

Flip the quilt top forward to position batting

Step 4 Begin to roll the quilt top onto the front roller. The top fabric needs to be wound securely around the roller, just like the backing was. The difference is that the top edge is not attached to anything yet – that comes later. An easy way to roll the quilt top up is to place the quilt top up and over the pick-up roller, and then wind it using the hand wheel. The quilt backing provides enough resistance that the wrinkles are pulled out, and the quilt top loads easily. Bulky seam lines will cause some shifting but the top should wind up straight.

Positioning the Batting

The batting is positioned between the two layers of fabric. When a roll of unfolded batting is stored on a pole under the table, it can be drawn off of the roll as the quilt is advanced. More commonly, the batting is pre-cut and packaged or measured and cut from a roll that is not stored on the pole under the table. Then the batting is cut to measure and placed on top of the backing, between the rollers. The top edge is aligned with the top of the backing and the excess falls to the floor.

Position batting between the layers

Step 1 Place the upper edge of the batting just below the pins in the pick-up leader.

Step 2 Place the quilt top over the batting, leaving about one inch of batting exposed at the top. You should still be able to see the canvas leader and the pins, which guarantees you won't hit them.

Position the batting and quilt top on the backing

Normally this is the time to secure the layers of your quilt by stitching across the top edge. If you know how to do this already, feel free to continue. However, if this is the first time you have loaded a quilt, you will need to learn a few more skills before you are ready to stitch. So, read through Securing the Stitches (page 50) and Tension and Stitch Quality (page 54) before attempting to secure the layers.

Securing the Layers

If you haven't already done so, now is the time to choose a thread color, wind some bobbins, thread the machine and test the stitch quality using the test sandwich.

Step 1 Position the sewing head in the center of the quilt, so the needle is a scant ¼" away from the upper edge of the quilt top.

Position the needle in the center at the top edge

Step 2 Check the positioning of the quilt top by engaging the horizontal channel lock and just moving the machine (not stitching) from the center to each side. Reposition the fabric if needed, to be sure the fabric is straight. When ready, you can stitch beginning at the center and moving out to the side. Repeat for the other side.

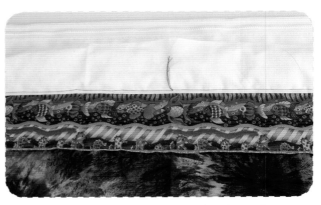

tip
When using the framing strips, be sure the basting stitches are on the strips, just outside the seam line.

Always stitch from the center to the side

Basting stitches should be on the framing strips

Step 3 Tighten up the quilt top when done and attach the side clamps. If the backing is wide enough, the clamps will be far enough away from the quilting surface that they won't interfere. If the clamps are too close, it is helpful to use a yardstick propped across the rollers and under the clamps to keep them elevated and prevent them from catching on the machine.

tip
Basting the sides is optional. The quilt construction and quilting designs selected will help determine if it is advisable to baste the sides. Using the vertical channel lock is a good way to be sure the sides aren't being stretched in either direction.

Basting the sides is recommended

Use yard sticks to elevate the clamps

Step 4 Check that the backing is not wrinkled and that is does not sag. Fix any wrinkles or sags now.

Advancing the Quilt

Step 1 Remove the side clamps. Loosen the tension on the quilt by releasing the locking levers on both the backing fabric (lower edge) and the quilt top fabric (lower edge). To do this, flip the locking lever over and away from the gear-like collar around the rollers.

Remove the locking lever from the backing and quilt top rollers

Step 2 Gently turn the hand wheel on the takeup roller. This will advance the quilt layers onto the takeup roller, bringing up the next section of quilt.

Step 3 Tighten the backing first by flipping the locking lever back onto the gearlike collar and turning the hand wheel. (On my machine, I turn it until the ratchety noise stops).

Check underneath for wrinkles and sags in backing

Step 4 Smooth the batting and quilt top with your hands, removing any wrinkles that might appear. Include the front facing area since that is where the wrinkles first appear.

Check for wrinkles in the batting

Step 5 Tighten the quilt top by flipping the locking lever back onto the gearlike collar and turning the handwheel (until the ratchety noise stops).

Step 6 Replace the side clamps and baste the sides if desired.

Step 7 Check the underside for wrinkles and sags.

 tip Don't get the fabric too taut or too loose! You should be able to push your finger up from underneath the quilt and grab onto the first digit with your other hand. If you can't do this, the fabric is too taut.

Securing the Stitches

A very important step in any quilting style is to secure the threads so the quilting does not come out. To secure threads by machine, both threads need to be on the top of the quilt and a knot is made. The knots are called tie-off stitches, and they are done at the beginning and the ending of a line of stitching.

At the Start of a Line of Quilting

Step 1 Hold the top thread securely and take one single stitch. Holding the top thread prevents it from being drawn down into the bobbin area.

Holding the top thread securely, take a single stitch

Step 2 Without letting go of the top thread, move the machine head away 6"-8". Notice that the bobbin thread is pulled up to the top of the quilt.

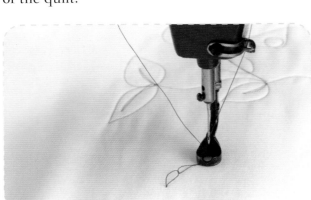

Move the machine away, exposing the bobbin-thread loop

Step 3 Hold both threads and return the machine head to the starting point. Holding the threads prevents them from getting knotted on the underside of the quilt.

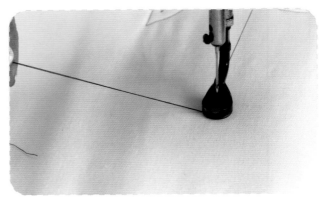

Bring the machine back to the first stitch

Step 4 Take four to five single stitches (called tie-off stitches), being sure to move the machine head a tiny bit between each stitch. Trim the thread tails when convenient.

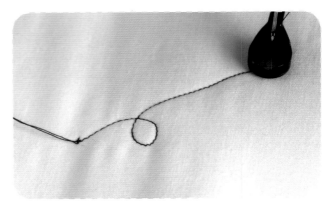

Begin stitching

tip Use a scissors with a blunt tip when trimming the threads to avoid puncturing the fabric.

At the End of a Line of Quilting

Step 1 Take four to five tie-off stitches to create a knot. Remember to move the machine head a tiny bit between each stitch.

Take four to five tie-off stitches

Step 2 Push the machine away about 6"-8". Grab the top thread and don't let go.

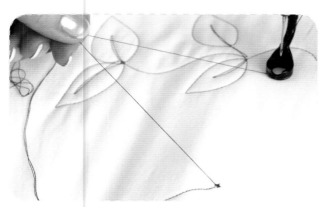

Move the machine away, about 6"-8" and grab the thread

Step 3 Bring the machine back to the last stitch, and take one single stitch in the same spot if possible. Still holding on to the top thread, push the machine away again. The bobbin thread comes to the top surface in a loop.

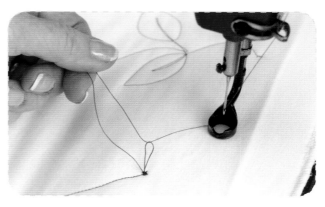

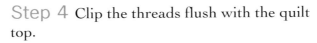

Step 4 Clip the threads flush with the quilt top.

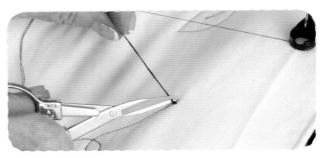

Clip the threads

Alternative Tie-off Method

Tie-off stitches do create a visible knot. The way to prevent knots from showing on the surface is to hand tie the knot and bury the thread tails with a needle. This is also the recommended method for hiding thread tails resulting from restarts caused by thread breaks or bobbin refills.

Step 1 Tie the thread tails in a double knot.

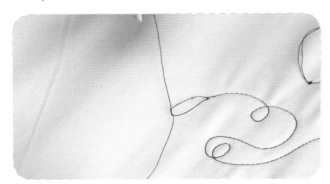

Tie a double knot

Step 2 Place the tip of the needle into the fabric next to the knot. Insert the needle partially, keeping it between the layers and leaving the eye of the needle exposed.

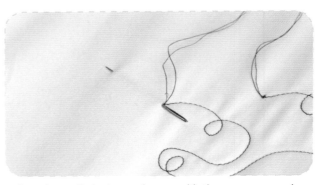

Insert needle between layers with the eye exposed

tip Don't try to be thrifty with your thread when doing the starts and stops. If you don't have long enough thread tails, you will find yourself wasting time because the top thread pulls out of the eye of the needle or the bobbin thread is so short that it can't be captured when beginning a line of stitching.

Step 3 Insert a needle threader into the eye of the needle and catch the threads. I recommend a hook-shaped needle threader.

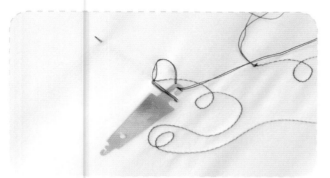

Use a needle threader to catch the threads

Step 4 Pull the threads through the eye.

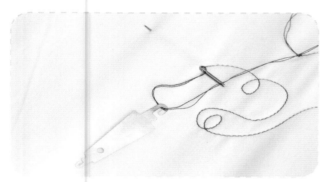

Pull thread tails through the eye

Step 5 Finish pushing the needle through the fabric, pulling the threads through the inner layers.

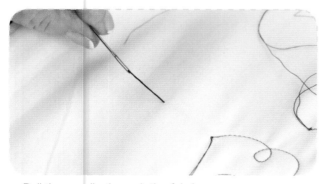

Pull the needle through the fabric

Step 6 Give a little tug on the threads to pop the knot into the batting. Clip the threads flush with the quilt top.

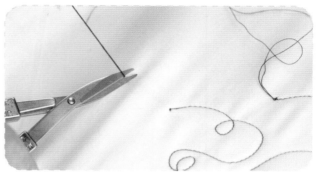

Pop the knot and clip the threads

tip Use a long, sharp needle with a large eye like a tapestry or couching needle. If you can't find a needle threader with a hook on it, get a tapestry needle threader and a tweezers to help get the threads through.

Many people use the machine to secure the stitches, and only do it by hand when necessary. Others routinely hand-tie knots and bury the threads using a needle and threader. Burying the knots by hand is preferred by many quilt judges. The photo below shows examples of both methods. The stitch line on top was secured with the machine. The stitch line on the bottom was tied and buried by hand.

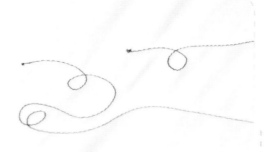

Knots made by machine are more obvious than those done by hand

Tension and Stitch Quality

Stitch quality is a result of several variables: the fabric, batting, thread, machine tension and quilt tautness. Before doing any quilting, it is a good idea to check the stitch quality and warm up by practicing on a test sandwich. Always check your stitch quality at the beginning of the quilt and every time you change the thread or bobbin.

tip Every time I change the bobbin, I clean out the bobbin area and use my test sandwich to check the tension, blot any residual oil, and catch any stray wads of gunk that I might have loosened.

tip Usually the top and bobbin thread will be the same color, but for testing the tension the first time, it might be helpful to have two different colors so you can really examine the stitch quality.

54

Making a Test Sandwich

MATERIALS
Two pieces of muslin approximately 12" long by the width of the fabric, about 42"
One piece of batting the same size
Domestic sewing machine or serger
Thread

Step 1 Layer the batting inside the two pieces of fabric and pin to hold the layers secure.

Finish three edges

It is a good idea to have several test (quilt) sandwiches, each with a different type of batting. By leaving one edge open, you will know which type you are using. The fabric and batting can affect stitch quality so try to use a test piece that contains the same type of fabric and batting as the quilt. One test sandwich will last for many quilts, depending on how much stitching you do to warm up.

Layer and pin

Step 2 Stitch around three sides.

basic skill

Using the Test Sandwich

Mount the test (quilt) sandwich by pinning it to the canvas leaders or, depending on your machine, by pinning it around the bars.

Step 1 Pin the test quilt sandwich to your machine so you can use both hands for quilting. Use the same thread you have chosen for the quilt.

The test sandwich spans the quilting area

Step 2 Take a single stitch and pull up the bobbin thread. Take some tie-off stitches if desired. Begin by stitching simple straight lines and curves.

Stitches should look balanced on curves and in lines

Step 3 Unpin one corner and look at the stitch quality on both sides. Examine the stitch, paying attention to how the top and bobbin threads are balanced. Adjust the tension if needed and test again.

Be sure the bobbin thread looks good, too

Step 4 Replace the pin so you have a flat quilting surface and begin stitching again. This time practice your free motion or your design. The test piece is a great place to find the rhythm of your quilting motion.

Practice the designs to get the feel of the machine

When ready, remove the quilt sandwich so it does not interfere when you roll your quilt.

Tension Problems

Pokies

Also known as pin-dotting, pokies come from unbalanced tension which results in too much thread from one side being visible on the other side. If the top thread is too tight, the pokies are visible on the top. If the top thread is too loose, the pokies are visible on the bottom. Pokies can rarely be completely eliminated, so using the same thread color on top and bottom is a good idea.

Eyelashing

Eyelashing is a more serious tension problem. Also known as railroad tracking, this occurs when the tension is seriously unbalanced. When eyelashing happens on one side, the thread on the other side needs to be adjusted. Eyelashing is usually more obvious on curves.

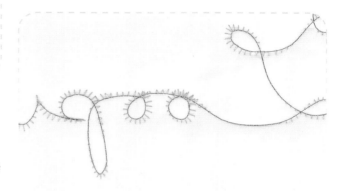

Eyelashing shows uneven tension on curves

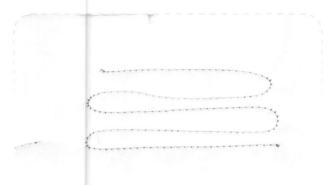

Pin-dotting is caused by unbalanced tension.

Loopies

Loopies usually happen when the check spring is broken or too loose. The stitch looks loose on top and it is twisted on the bottom.

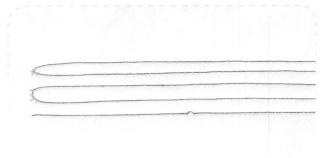

Loopies indicate the check spring needs adjusting

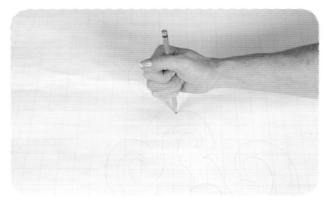

Hold the pencil as you would hold the machine handles

> **tip** It is possible to practice free-motion quilting using a large sheet of paper and pencil. Hold the pencil in your fist, not in your fingers as is customary. Place the paper on an elevated table or countertop and stand up to practice, just like you were standing in front of your machine so you practice with your arm muscles, not your finger muscles. I prefer flip-chart paper with a printed 1" grid so I can monitor my quilting scale.

Free-Motion Quilting

Free-motion quilting is done without a pattern, stencil or template. Each quilter has their own personal style of free-motion quilting, much like handwriting styles.

Free-motion quilting is done from the front of the machine. In theory, the quilter just imagines the design and stitches it directly onto the quilt top. In reality, we sometimes mark guidelines on the quilt top to help us maintain consistency. Unlike handwriting, quilting involves more of the body than just the hands. Training these muscles to express and control your own personal style takes practice.

When it comes to free-motion quilting, practice, practice and more practice will improve your ability to control your quilting. Machines with a stitch regulator might be easier to use because there is no need to control the machine speed while learning everything else.

Meandering Loops

Quilting a loop design is a good way to learn how to control the machine in all directions. Strive to make all the loops evenly sized and as circular as possible. The lines connecting the loops should be curved, not straight. The loops should fill the space without the appearance of rows. Alternating the direction of each loop (one clockwise and the next counterclockwise) helps improve control because it allows frequent direction changes. Fill the entire space as you go. If that is not possible, leave an uneven edge, not a straight one so the next section can blend in. The uneven edge is marked in the photo. Notice how the lower section fills in the uneven areas.

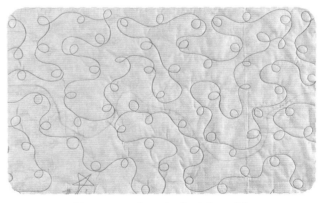

Loopy quilting can soften the look by adding curves

Loops and Five-Point Stars

Adding the star is a good way to learn how to include direction changes. The star points require bringing the machine to a complete stop and then moving again in a different direction with a smooth motion. Points will be rounded if the machine does not come to a complete stop. The star teaches how to plan the quilting route also. Notice that the star entry and exit directions are opposite. The loops become a transitional element of the design, allowing direction changes. Sometimes it is helpful to draw the stars onto the practice piece so you don't work yourself into a corner.

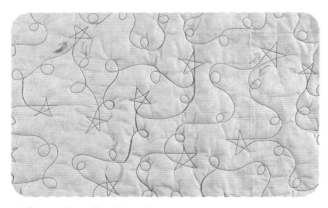

Stars allow direction changes

Stippling

Another technique that has evolved from hand quilting is stippling. Good stippling is usually very small, has no straight line segments and absolutely no crossing over. Large-scale stippling is also called meandering. Regardless of the scale, be consistent in the distance between quilting lines and keep all quilting curvy.

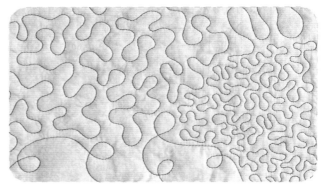

Stippling is tiny meandering

tip I have zipper leaders on my machine, and I had an extra set of zippers. So I made a test quilt. I used several yards of fabric for both the top and backing, and I used some leftover scraps for the batting. When I need to practice a new design, I zip on the test quilt and practice until I am comfortable.

Leaves

A simple leaf is a combination of straight lines, start and stops and left and right curves. Quilting leaves might feel more like drawing than quilting, which is the objective! Make the leaf by beginning with the center spine. This requires coming to a complete stop and changing direction. At the top of the leaf make a curve in one direction, stitch toward the bottom of the leaf, aim to make the leaf point somewhere past the end of the center spine and at the point, change direction and try to make a mirror image of the leaf along the other side.

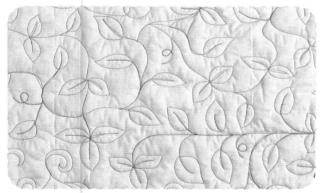

Leaves don't need to be identical and can be grouped

Echo Stitching

This is an extremely useful technique. Echo stitching enhances a focal point by outlining it. At the same time, it can fill the background without detracting from the focal point. Most machines have a quarter inch between the tip of the needle and any point on the outer edge of the hopping foot so there is a built-in guide. By moving the machine so the outer edge of the hopping foot moves along an existing stitch line or seam line, the line is echoed. Using an echo stitch technique can transform a quilting design into a beautiful filler, as seen when the C curl is echo quilted.

Echo stitch the C curls for a beautiful filler

Curls and Swirls

Soft swirly quilting designs add motion to a quilt and balance the lines inherent in patchwork. A simple curl is shaped like the letter C. The stitch line flows into the curl with the inside arc, stops and changes direction, completing the outside arc. The curl is completed by a crossover or another change in stitch direction.

Curls add motion

Pantograph Quilting

A popular type of edge-to-edge quilting is done with a pattern called a pantograph. Pantographs are usually rolled paper patterns that are placed on the table bed, under a protective sheet of plastic. The pattern is traced using a stylus or laser light with the quilter standing at the back of the machine. The stitching is a continuous-line design, repeated across the area from edge to edge.

Edge-to-edge (E2E) patterns in their simplest forms are continuous line designs that, when stitched in multiple repeats, create a pleasing overall design. Some have a particular motif and the motifs are joined by connecting lines that frequently create secondary designs. The most complicated pantographs are made up of multiple pattern rows that, when stitched together, create a mural-like design.

When a pantograph has distinctive linear top and bottom edges, it can be used for a border area. Many even come with a complementary corner design which makes the direction change a smooth transition. Resizing edge-to-edge patterns can be a challenge, so sometimes the border pantographs are offered in multiple heights.

Border patterns often have corner pieces

tip Avoid buying patterns that contain perfect lines, circles or any other symmetrical shapes. Perfection is hard to attain and imperfect symmetrical shapes are very obvious.

tip When using a design that doesn't fit the quilt perfectly, consider adding framing strips to the quilt top. They enable you to quilt off the edges without causing tucks and puckers.

Pantograph patterns often show dotted lines for positioning the next row

Stitching a Pantograph

There are many "right" ways to stitch a pantograph. The instructions here are based on my experiences as a teacher, and they are conservative. Over time you will develop your own technique, and your way will be the "right" way, too!

Terms

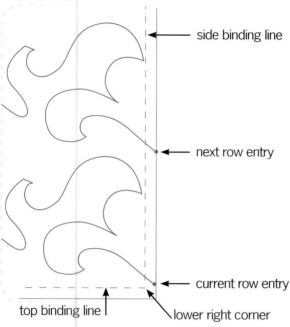

side binding line

next row entry

current row entry

lower right corner

top binding line

Binding Line

The line where the binding will be sewn to the quilt. Anything to the outside of this line is either trimmed away or buried in the binding.

Lower Right Corner

The intersection of the top and side binding lines. If you stand at the front of the machine, this would be the upper left corner. Since pantographs are stitched from the back of the machine, we call it the Lower Right Corner. This is the side we will begin each row of quilt stitching.

Lower Left Corner

The intersection of the top and side Binding Lines, but on the side where we will end each row of stitching.

Current Row Entry Point

The point on the pattern where stitching begins for the current row.

Current Row Ending Point

The point on the pattern where the stitching ends for the current row.

Next Row Entry Point

The point on the pattern where stitching would begin for the "next" row. It is used to make adjustments to the laser-light positioning when advancing from one row to the next.

Net Row Height

The distance between the Current and Next Row Entry Points. The Net Row Height is determined by the height of one single row, adjusted for the amount of space between the rows. If the rows are nested, the Net Row Height is less than the height of one single row.

Steps for Stitching a Pantograph

Get the Machine and Table Ready

Step 1.1 Turn on the power and lights.

Step 1.2 Wipe the needle area, removing any lint or residual oil.

Step 1.3 Move the laser light to its mount in the back of the machine, and turn it on.

Step 1.4 Select the thread, wind bobbins and thread the machine.

Step 1.5 Always use a test sandwich to check the stitch quality.

Use a test sandwich to check the stitch quality

Load and Position the Quilt

Step 2.1 Load the backing, batting and quilt top.

Step 2.2 Baste the top edge using the horizontal channel lock to be sure it is square.

Step 2.3 Baste the side edges using the vertical channel lock.

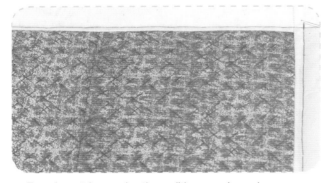

Framing strips make the quilting much easier

Get the Pattern Ready

Step 3.1 Place the pattern on the table under the protective plastic sheet.

Step 3.2 If the pattern is directional, check that the direction matches the quilt. This step is easy to forget, because the pattern might seem upside down when standing at the back of the machine.

Step 3.3 Use the registration marks on the tabletop to check that the pattern is straight.

Mark the Beginning Binding Line

Step 4.1 Look at your quilt top and decide where the top and side Binding Lines will be. Move the machine head to the Lower Right Corner of the quilt (which is the intersection of the two Binding Lines on the beginning side). Put the needle in the down position here.

Step 4.2 Look at your pattern, and decide where the Binding Line will be. Choose a place on the pattern (usually between motifs) that would be a good place to begin stitching. Place a strip of masking tape on the plastic that is covering the pattern, positioned so it is perpendicular to the table track and overlaps the place where the Binding Line will be.

Step 4.3 On this piece of tape, mark the top and side Binding Lines. The intersection of the two Binding Lines is the Lower Right Corner. Mark and label the Lower Right Corner on the tape and adjust the laser light (or stylus) to point to this spot. You have now aligned the quilt top to the pattern.

Beginning Binding Lines

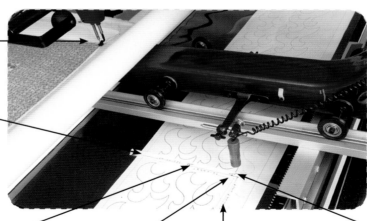

Step 4.1
Needle **down** at lower right corner

Step 4.2
Masking tape identifies where the side binding line is

Step 7.1
Mark the Next Row entry point

Step 6.1
Mark the Current Row entry point

Step 4.3
Masking tape identifies where the top binding line is

Step 4.4
Align the laser light to this point. Label it Lower Right Corner

Mark the Ending Binding Line

Step 5.1 Raise the needle, and move the machine head to the Lower Left Corner of the quilt. Put the needle in the down position here.

Step 5.2 Notice where the laser light is pointing on the pattern. This point is on the opposite Binding Line. Place a strip of masking tape on the plastic covering the pattern, perpendicular to the table track, overlapping the place where the Binding Line will be.

Step 5.3 On this piece of tape, mark the top and side Binding Lines. The intersection of the two Binding Lines is the Lower Left Corner. Mark this point on the tape, too.

> **tip** If you would like to reposition the pattern, now is the time. The Binding Lines represent the side edges of the quilt, so move the pantograph pattern until it fits between the side Binding Lines and looks attractive. When done, be sure to verify that the pattern is still parallel with the leaders and the alignment is still correct.

Ending Binding Lines

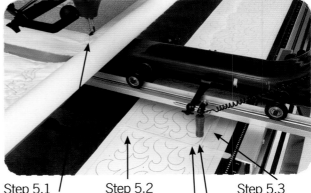

Step 5.1 Needle **down** at lower left corner

Step 5.2 Masking tape identifies where the ending side binding is

Step 5.3 Masking tape identifies where the top binding is

Step 5.5 Current Row End Point

Step 5.4 Label this the Lower Left Corner

Mark the Current Row Entry Point

Step 6.1 Raise the needle, and move the machine back to the beginning Binding Line. Find the point on the pattern where the Binding Line intersects the first row. On the masking tape, make a dot about ⅛" outside of the Binding Line and label it "Current Row Entry."

Mark the Next Row Entry Point

Step 7.1 If the pattern has two rows on it, find the point on the pattern where the Binding Line intersects the second row. On the masking tape, make a dot about ⅛" outside of the Binding Line and label it "Next Row Entry." The distance between the "current" and "next" row entry points is the Net Row Height.

Alternative Method: If the pattern only shows one row you must find the "Next Row Entry." Determine the Net Row height and measure this distance along the masking tape and label this point.

Check the Positioning Before Stitching

Step 8.1 Move the machine head so the laser is pointing to the Current Row Entry Point. The needle should be pointing just outside of the Binding Line.

Step 8.2 Without stitching, move the machine so the laser follows the pattern. Pause at the highest and lowest spots in the pattern and check the alignment.

Step 8.3 Move the machine to the end of the row and check the positioning. When the laser is on the Current Row Ending Point marked on the tape, the needle should be past the Binding Line of the quilt. Make adjustments if needed.

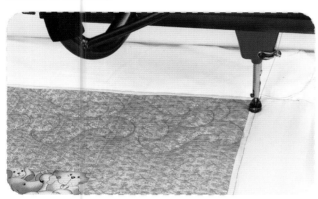

When the laser is on the tape, the needle should be past the Binding Line

tips
• Take sliding steps when moving from one side to the next. Gently shift your weight from one foot to the other to minimize any interruptions in the flow.

• Relax your grip on the machine, and don't forget to breath!

• Avoid back fatigue by maintaining good posture.

• If you need to pause, do it in an inconspicuous spot, like a point.

Stitch the First Row of the Design

Step 9.1 Return the laser light to the Current Row Entry Point.

Step 9.2 Take one stitch to bring up the bobbin thread and take four or five tie-off stitches, being sure the knot will be hidden in the binding area.

Step 9.3 Begin to stitch in one continuous smooth flow, working to the other side.

Step 9.4 Stop when the laser light meets the Current Row End Point, which should be at or past the Binding Line.

Step 9.5 Take five locking stitches, being sure the knot is in the binding area.

Step 9.6 Pull up the bobbin thread, and cut the thread tails.

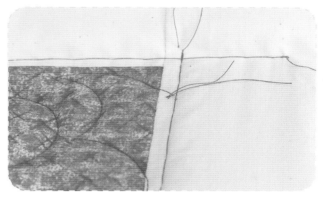

The tie-off knot is just past the Binding Line

Reposition the Machine for the Next Row

Step 10.1 Move the machine head back to the Beginning Binding Line and put the laser light on the Next Row Entry Point. Put the needle in the down position.

Step 10.2.A If there is enough quilting space to do another row:

1. Leave the needle where it is and move the laser light to the Current Row Entry Point.

2. Raise the needle and check the positioning before stitching (Step 8). Be sure the second row stitching does not overlap the first row.

3. When ready to stitch the next row, repeat Step 9.

Step 10.2.B If there is not space enough to do another row:

1. Pick up the needle and put a pin in the quilt top to mark the spot.

2. Roll the quilt.

3. Position the machine head over the start-point pin.

4. Remove the pin and put the needle down.

5. Realign the laser light so it is pointing at the This Row Entry Point on the masking tape.

6. Raise the needle and check the positioning before stitching (Step 8).

7. Be sure the second row stitching does not overlap the first row.

8. When ready to stitch the next row, repeat Step 9.

tip Sometimes the Entry and Exit points need to be adjusted. This is common because some quilts get wider or thinner in the middle. Just watch the lines and make adjustments as needed.

Step 11 Repeat Step 10 until the last row.

Stitch the Last Row

When measuring the quilt and the design to see if they will match, you have three options to consider for stitching the last row.

Option 1

If the pantograph design fits the quilt perfectly, finish the last row by following the steps above.

Option 2

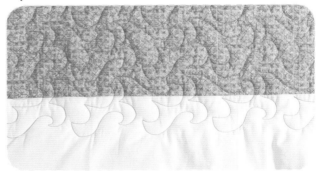

Sometimes the pantograph design extends past the bottom edge of the quilt, but you can stitch off the edge because you added framing strips and you have enough backing fabric. In this case, finish the last row by following the steps above. You will stitch off the edge of the quilt, but that is OK.

Option 3

Sometimes the pantograph design extends past the bottom edge of the quilt, and you can't stitch off the edge because there are not framing strips or there is not enough backing fabric.

Be sure to remove the pins and/or zipper leader from the quilt top. Baste this bottom edge down so it doesn't get flipped over when stitching off the edge. Keep the basting stitches very close to the edge of the quilt top if possible .

Move the machine so the needle is on the basting stitches at the bottom. Look at the pattern and notice where the laser light is pointing. Place a piece of masking tape on the plastic sheet which is covering the pattern that aligns with the laser light. Use this as a boundary when quilting. It can be tricky, but it is possible to quilt just part of the pantograph, and when you get to the taped boundary, stitch along the taped edge to the next part of the pattern. Repeat across the last row.

Use tape to mark the bottom edge of the quilt

tips

•When you break a thread or run out of bobbin thread (and you will!) try to restart in an inconspicuous spot, too. Sometimes this means ripping out stitches and backing up to a point or intersection.

•Burying the thread tails with a needle is a very effective way to make the restart (almost) invisible.

Stencils and Templates

Stencils and templates have been used in quilting for years. Both techniques enable a quilter to mark a quilt with the design before quilting. Stencils and templates require more control of the quilting machine, which is why these techniques are considered the next level.

A stencil is a sheet of metal, paper or plastic that has channels cut into it. The channels are wide enough for a marking pen, pencil, chalk pounce pad or chalk dispenser to mark the line that creates the design. The quilter then follows the marked line to stitch the design.

Templates are also used to mark design lines; but instead of channels, the line is marked around the outer edge. A template can be a common geometric shape (like a circle made from the outline of a plate or glass), or it can be an original (you create your own design and cut out the shape from paper or plastic) or it can be a special shape that is custom made (laser cut from quarter-inch acrylic) to be used with a longarm machine. A ruler is a template that has a straight-line design.

Templates that are custom made for quilting systems also have the benefit of being a guide for the quilter. They can be placed on the quilt top and held in position with one hand while the other hand guides the quilting machine along the edge of the template. This eliminates the need to pre-mark the quilt top, which saves time. It also ensures a smoother stitch line because the template offers more stability resulting in more accurate quilting.

tip Beginners are surprised that they can mark a quilt accurately, but they can't quilt that line with the same accuracy. With practice you will train your arm muscles to gain more control. Don't be afraid to try different positions. An alternative to using only your arm muscles is to hold your arms stiff, and let your legs and torso direct the machine.

Using Stencils

tip Avoid choosing a stencil with perfect geometric shapes because they are very hard to execute. For example, a stencil design that consists of perfect circles will be very difficult to do. Templates are a better choice for a design that needs perfect geometric shapes.

Choose stencils that are continuous-line designs. If the stencil doesn't fit the space exactly, it is possible to modify the stencil to stretch certain design elements if needed to fill the space. This can be done either by cutting additional channels in the stencil, or by changing the markings after the stencil has been traced onto the quilt top.

Mark the quilt top and stitch. When marking, include any of the improvements you made. If needed, add arrows to remind you of the design path and direction. Take the time to stand back and look at just the marked quilting lines. Will the density of the stencil's quilted lines be consistent with the quilting designs chosen for the rest of the quilt top?

If the stencil is too large, modify your markings to fit

tip The first block I choose is never the middle block of the first row. I know without a doubt that the first stencil I stitch will not be my best one, so I start with an inconspicuous block.

71

Using Templates

Use an extended base plate if possible. The purpose of this plate is to expand the area around the needle and foot so you can control a template better. Without an extended base plate the template tends to wobble.

Hold the template with your fingers touching the fabric

Practice holding the template with your fingertips also touching the fabric. By doing this you can instantly feel the ruler if it slips. By teaching yourself to hold the template so that your fingers are touching the quilt top, you will be able to feel the ruler and stop stitching if it begins to move. Your fingers should be no more than six inches away from the hopping foot. Any further than that and the fingers won't hold the ruler securely enough to prevent any sliding. So, teach yourself to move your grip frequently, keeping the fingers close to the needle and hopping foot. Some people prefer to stop the machine before they move their grip and others practice how to walk their fingers along the ruler, keeping the distance less than six inches. I suggest trying both.

> **tip**
> Switch hands and stitching directions when practicing with templates. Sometimes when stitching around a template, it is necessary to switch from the one hand to the other. Similarly, it will be necessary to stitch clockwise and counter-clockwise so practice, practice, practice so you aren't "directionally challenged."

Straight Edge Ruler

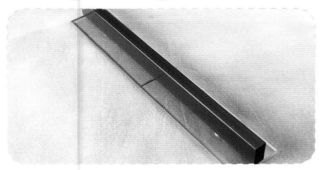

The best ones have a handle (so they are easier to hold), are made of a clear material (that enables you to see through it and make sure you are positioning the ruler properly) and have guide lines in ¼" increments etched on them. The ¼" markings are very useful when doing echo stitching because there is no need to mark the line for the echo stitching when the measuring guide is built into the ruler. The straight edge is essential when doing stitch-in-the-ditch detailing.

Circular Templates

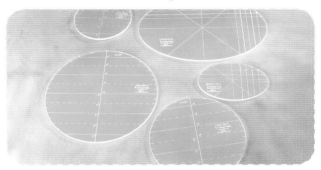

These are generally available in multiple sizes and are made of one sheet of acrylic, with concentric circles cut in them. Oval shapes are handy too, but squares and triangles really don't add enough value to offset the difficulty of storing them. Squares and triangles are very easy to do with the straight edge template instead.

Wavy Curve Templates

These are soft undulating curves that can be used individually or in combinations. They are used to make the pumpkin seed quilting design that is popular on Lone Star or Irish Chain patterns, and they make perfect spines for feathered blocks or borders.

Scalloped Edges

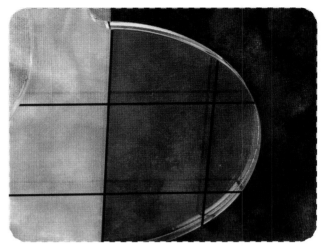

These are equally sized arcs that can also be used individually or in combinations. Imagine several scallop templates with the same repeat length, but different heights (amplitudes). When stitched together, they make a perfect swag design.

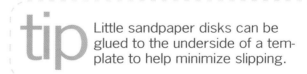

tip
Little sandpaper disks can be glued to the underside of a template to help minimize slipping.

out of this world

Shop-Hop Expandable Tote Bag

This tote bag is perfect for a shop hop because it can be folded in, making it only 18" tall for the beginning of the day. As you add treasures, it expands up to 35" tall.

Materials
1 yd. top fabric, 42"-44" wide
1 yd. backing fabric, 42"-44" wide
1 yd. batting, 38" x 46"
6 yd. webbing for handles, 1" wide
    cut into 2 long pieces (2½ yd) and
    4 short pieces (9" each)
⅛ yd. binding fabric

Free-motion quilting requires practice. Most of us do a better job when we practice on a good piece of fabric, not just scribbling on muslin.

For the outside of the quilt tote, I recommend a large print that won't show the tiny quilting details. The inside should be a plain fabric that does show the details. When you load the fabric on your table, treat the outside fabric like the backing and the inside fabric like the quilt top. Choose a thread color that blends with the outside fabric but contrasts with the inside fabric so you can really see what you are quilting.

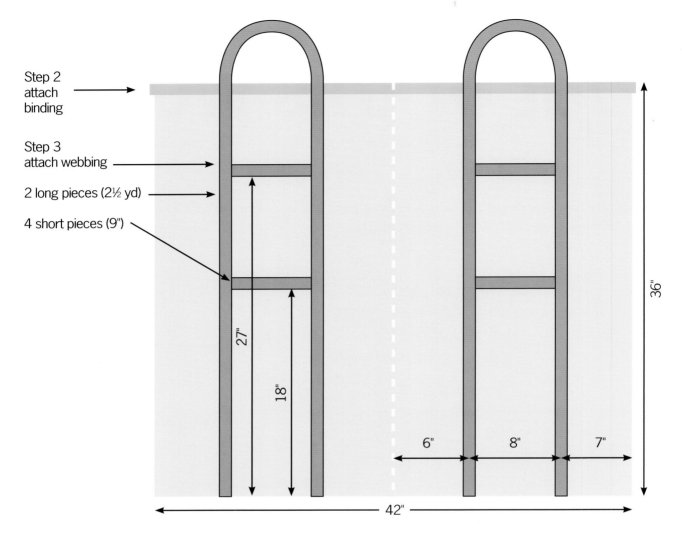

Step 2
attach
binding

Step 3
attach webbing

2 long pieces (2½ yd)

4 short pieces (9")

27"

18"

36"

6"   8"   7"

42"

Step 1 Load the fabric, backing and batting on your longarm. Practice any technique, attempting to quilt the fabric with consistent density. When done, square up the quilt, creating a rectangle. The short side will be about 36" and the long side will be about 42".

Practice any technique

Step 2 Prepare one strip of binding 44" long and 2½" wide. Use your favorite method to attach the binding to one of the long sides. This is the top edge.

Step 3 Position the long pieces of webbing on the quilt as shown. The cut ends should align with the bottom edge of the tote and will make handles at the top edge. Pin in place.

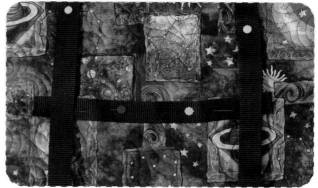

Webbing placement

Step 5 Position the short pieces of webbing on the quilt as shown on the diagram. The cut ends should tuck under the long pieces. When the long webbing pieces are stitched, the raw edges of the short pieces will be covered and secured. Because the short pieces are secured at the ends only, they create additional handles when the bag is folded in. Sew both the long webbing pieces, stitching about ⅛" from the edges.

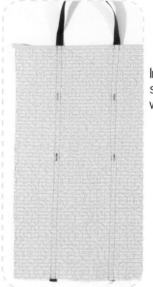

Inside view showing top stitching that holds the webbing in place

Step 4 Position the short pieces of webbing on the quilt as shown on the diagram. The cut ends should tuck under the long pieces. When the long webbing pieces are stitched, the raw edges of the short pieces will be covered and secured. Because the short pieces are secured at the ends only, they create additional handles when the bag is folded in. Sew both the long webbing pieces, stitching about ⅛" from the edges.

Step 6 Fold the bag right sides together and stitch from the bound edge toward the bottom and then across the bottom. Clean finish the seams with a serger or an overlock stitch.

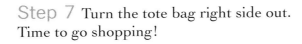
Step 7 Turn the tote bag right side out.
Time to go shopping!

let's go!

Show-and-Tell Quilt Carrier

This carrier is terrific for carrying your large, rolled quilts to show and tell at your quilt guild. Like the Shop-Hop Bag, this project will allow you to practice your free-motion stitching.

For the outside of the quilt tote, I recommend a large print that won't show the tiny quilting details. The inside should be a plain fabric that does show the details. When you load the fabric on your table, treat the outside fabric like the backing and the inside fabric like the quilt top. Choose a thread color that blends with the outside fabric but contrasts with the inside fabric so you can really see what you are quilting.

Materials
1 yd. top fabric, 42"-44" wide
1 yd. backing fabric, 42"-44" wide
1 yd. batting, 38" x 46"
(2) 24" dowels, ⅜" or ½" diameter
4 yd. cording for ties
2 yd. webbing for handles, 1" or 1½" wide
¾ yd. accent fabric for dowel pockets, cord tube and binding.

From the accent fabric, cut:
2 strips, 2½" x 26" (dowel pockets)
2 strips, 2" x 37" (cord tubes)
4 strips, 2½" x width of fabric for binding

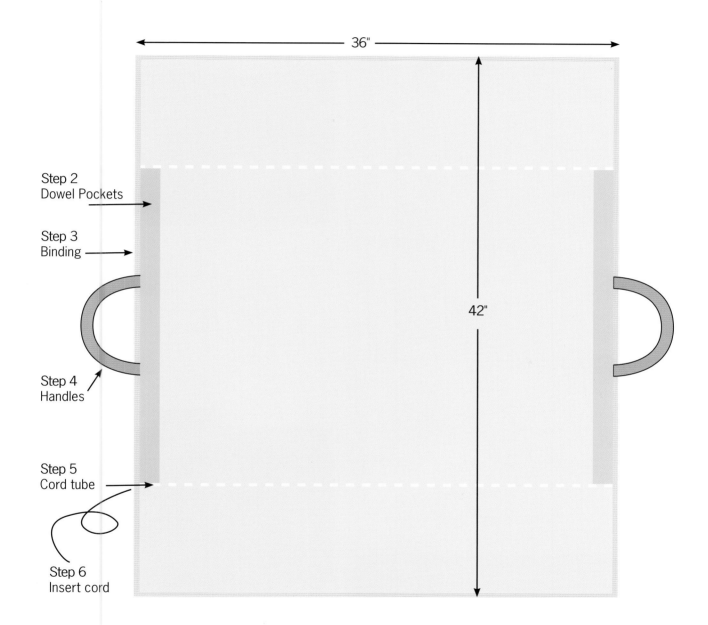

36"

42"

Step 2
Dowel Pockets

Step 3
Binding

Step 4
Handles

Step 5
Cord tube

Step 6
Insert cord

Step 1 Load the fabric, backing and batting on your longarm. Practice any technique, attempting to quilt the fabric with consistent density. When done, square up the quilt creating a rectangle. The short side will be about 36" and the long side will be about 42".

Step 2 Create a pocket for the dowels: Using the two 26" strips of accent fabric, press under ¼" along one long edge. Place the other long edge of the accent fabric on the dark side of the quilted fabric, centered on the long side, and matching the raw edges. Baste in place, a scant ¼" from the raw edge. Top stitch the other long edge keeping the stitching close to the folded edge. Leave the short ends open.

Step 3 Prepare the binding. Bind the entire perimeter being sure to catch the raw edges of the dowel pocket in the binding. (This is also a good time to practice applying and topstitching the binding by machine.)

Step 4 Create the handles. Cut the webbing into two 1-yard pieces. Baste them onto the quilted fabric, about 1" (inside) from the ends of the dowel pocket. (See photo for placement.) When done, fold the handles over and reinforce by stitching through the handle, binding and quilted layers. Be careful not to stitch across the dowel pocket.

Handle placement

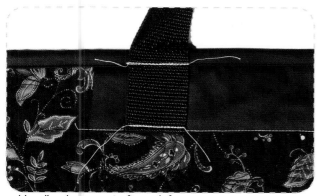

Handle placement after reinforcement

Step 5 Create a tube for the cord: The tube must have both ends hemmed so the fabric does not fray, but measure the space first to make sure it will fit exactly. Refer to the illustration or photos for positioning. The tube should begin and end exactly at the binding, and cover the exposed raw edges of the dowel pocket. After the tube is measured, trimmed (if needed) and hemmed, press under ¼" along both long edges. Position the strips on the quilt as shown in the diagram and pin. Topstitch one side in place. Insert the dowel and then topstitch the other side.

Step 6 Thread the cord through the tube. Use a safety pin to help insert the cord into the tube.

star light, star bright

Super Simple Quilt

Make your life simpler by taking advantage of the fabulous cotton prints that are available to-day. This quilt top can be assembled in about an hour which makes it a great choice for practic-ing quilting techniques. This pattern is also a great choice for charity quilts. By using fabulous fabric, no one will notice that it is a one-patch block!

Material
1¾ yd. focus fabric, 42"-44" wide
1¾ yd. border fabric, 42"-44" wide
3½ yd. backing fabric, 42"-44" wide
Batting, 1 twin size package

Finished Size: 80" x 63"

There are only two fabrics needed for the quilt top. One fabric will be the focus fabric. Choose a medium to large-scale print that has lots of color and interest. This will be the one-patch center of the quilt. The second fabric should be a complementary color or small-scale print that will border the focus fabric. This fabric will also be used for binding.

Choose a solid, tone-on-tone or marbled fabric for the backing. If you have pre-washed the quilt-top fabrics, it is wise to pre-wash the backing also.

For the thread, choose a color that will be a contrast to the backing. This will help you to see the stitches better when quilting and checking the stitch quality.

Cut:

1 piece focus fabric, 60½" x 40½". Trim off the selvage edges

2 strips border fabric, 60½" x 6½" (side borders)

2 strips border fabric, 52½" x 6½" (top/bottom borders)

4 strips border fabric, 63" x 2½" (binding)

(Cut the border and binding strips lengthwise – along the grain)

2 pieces backing fabric, 62" x width of fabric. Trim the selvage and seam the two together creating the backing which measures approximately 80" x 62".

Piecing Instructions

Step 1 Sew the two side borders onto the main focus fabric.

Step 2 Sew the top and bottom borders onto the quilt top.

Step 3 Square up the quilt top if needed.

Quilting Instructions

Step 1 Add framing strips to stabilize the quilt edges.

Add framing strips

tip If the thread blends into the focus fabric but contrasts with the backing, and the plan is to quilt a random overall design, consider loading the quilt upside down to make it easier to see what you are quilting.

Step 2 Choose a thread color and wind bobbins.

Step 3 Load the three quilt layers on your longarm. Thread the machine and check the stitch quality on a test sandwich piece. Adjust the tension if needed.

Step 4 Quilt as desired. Choose a quilting design that complements the quilt. Try to keep the quilting density consistent throughout the entire quilt.

tip Some people tend to quilt smaller scale as they progress down a quilt and some get larger. The change is so gradual that you may not notice until you are done with the quilting. To avoid this, quilt the first section and before rolling it, trace your quilting design on a piece of paper. This will be your target scale for the whole quilt. Keep the paper on the quilt top surface so you can glance at it as you quilt. This will ensure consistent quilting density.

Step 5 When done quilting, remove the quilt from the table, remove the zippers or pins and trim the quilt.

Binding Instructions

Step 1 Using a domestic-sewing machine, join the binding strips making one long binding strip.

Step 2 Press the strip in half lengthwise, wrong sides together.

Step 3 If the binding will be finished by hand, attach the binding to the quilt top side of the quilt. If finishing by machine, attach the binding to the backing side of the quilt. Fold over and finish the binding by hand or machine.

tip For detailed instructions describing how to apply binding, look in your favorite quilting magazine. They usually have a section that explains each step in the quilting process.

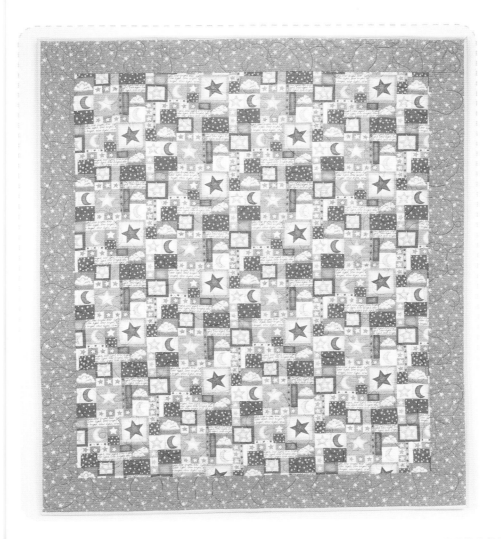

autumn leaves

Recliner Quilt

This is a quick and easy quilt to make for someone who has a special chair, usually a recliner. Many people who have favorite recliners are known to fall asleep during the football games, so why not make him a quilt that is only as wide as the chair, but that reaches from his nose to his toes?

Materials

10 fat quarters of assorted prints or colors
for blocks
2½ yd. backing fabric, 42"-44" wide
¾ yd. binding fabric, 42"-44" wide
Batting, 1 twin size package

Finished Size: 80" x 40"

The backing fabric is the focus fabric in this quilt. Choose a pattern that is masculine or that suits the recipient's personal interests. Once the backing has been selected, choose ten fat quarters (or any scraps from your stash) that complement the backing. They can be any pattern or color. Flannel is often a good choice. Choose a binding fabric that also complements the backing.

Pressing direction:

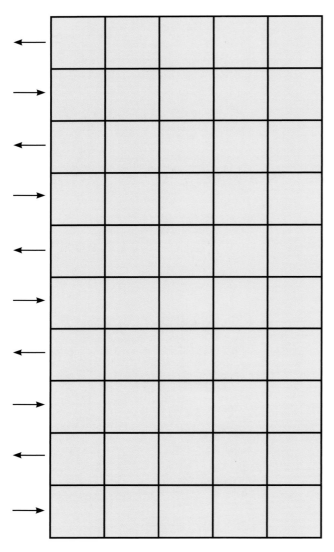

Cut:

50 blocks, 8½" by 8½" for quilt top

9 strips binding fabric, 2½" x width of fabric

Backing fabric, square up the piece if needed, but keep it one piece.

Piecing Instructions

Step 1 Use a design wall if possible to position the quilt blocks in a pleasing manner.

Step 2 Stitch the blocks together in rows. Press seam allowances in opposite directions every other row.

Step 3 Stitch the rows together to complete the quilt top.

tip By pressing the seam allowances in opposite directions every other row, matching the seams when joining the rows is easy. At each seam intersection, the bulk of the seam allowances locks together aligning the seams.

Quilting Instructions

Step 1 Add framing strips to secure the side seams and to stabilize the edges of the quilt top.

Add framing strips

Step 2 Choose a thread color and wind bobbins.

Step 3 Load the three quilt layers on your longarm. Thread the machine and check the stitch quality on a test sandwich piece. Adjust the tension if needed.

Step 4 Quilt as desired. Choose a quilting design that complements the quilt. Try to keep the quilting density consistent throughout the entire quilt.

Step 5 When done quilting, remove the quilt from the table, remove the zippers or pins and trim the quilt.

Commercial
Confidence

This third section recommends ways to build confidence by improving your own quilting abilities, developing good relationships with other quilters and creating a solid reputation in the quilting community.

For people who choose to start a business there is a section on things to consider as you develop your plans, including how to set prices. Even if being a business owner does not appeal to you, this section contains valuable information on how to network with other quilters and accelerate your learning curve.

Building Personal Skills

There is no substitute for practice. Fortunately, there are ways to augment that practice time and become inspired by other people, techniques and designs. Inspiration comes from many sources and can take your quilting to the next level.

Attend shows and take photos

Quilt shows are a source of awesome inspiration and education. Find out if photography is allowed, and if it is, take your camera! For quilts that catch my eye, I like to take one picture of the full quilt, and then more photos of the quilting details.

Take Classes

There are many good quilting teachers throughout the world. Finding classes for longarm machine quilters is more challenging than finding a class for domestic-machine quilters, but they do exist. Some large quilt shows offer classes, and some quilt artists offer classes in their personal studios. Some techniques (like thread painting) are possible on any machine, so be sure to consider tak-

ing classes from people who don't work on a longarm or platform machine. When the class is over, experiment with adapting your skill to work with your machine.

Shop the Shows

At shows, look for trends in fabrics, colors, embellishments and techniques. Look especially at the quilt kits. If you detect a trend, consider what type of quilting will enhance the style of that trend. You can also then shop for patterns, stencils and thread colors that fit the trend. Do not photograph the products in a vendor's booth without explicit permission.

Sketch and Doodle

Interesting quilting designs exist almost everywhere, and if you sketch them when you see them you are more likely to remember them. If you are drawn to nature, look to the outdoors. When you are indoors, look for patterns in fabrics, upholstery, carpeting, wallpaper, tiled floors and even architectural details. Doodling helps to take the sketch, modify it to fit a continuous curve line and then commit it to memory.

Make an Inspiration Album

Many of the great ideas generated by the shows are forgotten over time, so make an inspiration album. Include the dated photos, sketches and notes you have collected.

I have a bulletin board in my studio, and I post photos of quilting styles and techniques that I want to try soon. By having them clearly visible, I am reminded to practice that style. When done, the photos go into my inspiration album.

tip When you have developed your own designs to your satisfaction, make a sampler quilt. Fill a small area with enough of each design so that other people will be able to visualize what that design would look like on their quilt. Be sure to bind your sampler quilt when done. When it is folded and stored in your studio, it looks like a real quilt, not just a test piece.

Do Charity Quilts

There are many organizations that help needy people who would appreciate your quilts for practical reasons. Consider accepting donated quilt tops and quilting them yourself. Use your inspiration album to select a quilting design suitable for the quilt top or use whatever technique you need to practice. Try your best, but don't be upset if the final product isn't quite professional grade. Remember that charity quilts are also a great place to practice applying binding and finishing by machine (on a domestic machine, not a longarm or platform machine).

Building Relationships

There are many talented people in the quilting community. Each quilter has taken a different path to get to where they are today, and most are happy to share their story. Many stories have been recorded in the major quilting publications for all to read. Networking with other quilters enables us to be both students and teachers.

tip Publications are a wonderful source of information describing the current quilting trends. They are rich with articles, ideas, patterns and inspiration. Advertising allows us to keep up with the new products.

The Internet

For people who like to spend time on the computer, the Internet might be considered more valuable than hard-copy publications.

Be careful, there is no guarantee that what you read is 100% accurate. As an example, there is a discussion group called the Longarm List that is open to anyone. Members post questions, and other members post answers. You will probably receive many answers, but you have no idea if they are right. If several people give similar answers, you can be pretty sure that the answer is a good one.

Join a Local Quilt Guild

Joining a guild is a good way to find out what the quilters in your area are doing. Sometimes there will be multiple guilds in an area. Quilt guilds usually offer some type of education. It might be a lecture by a featured speaker or it may be a hands-on project that the group participates in. Most guilds have some type of ongoing civic project like collecting quilts from the membership for charities. Sometimes the guild will sponsor a quilt show, and sometimes they might arrange for trips to attend quilt shows. Whatever the scope, it is a great way to meet people who have interests similar to yours. If you choose to become a professional quilter, these people are probably your target market, too.

Join Professional Organizations

Professional organizations can offer a larger perspective of the quilting community. They normally have greater exposure and attract a broader artistic base. The professional organizations usually distribute a publication that contains information of interest to a broad group of quilters. It generally has articles on artistic techniques, business management, product trends, show schedules and profiles of well-known quilt artists.

Attend Shows and Volunteer

Volunteering to help at quilt shows is a great way to learn more about perspective and appeal. If you are able to help with the judging by being a scribe, you will learn what a judge looks for. You will also see first hand the differences between two quilts, as seen through the judge's eyes. Similarly, you will learn what the public looks for if you volunteer to be a white-glove attendant. These people are assigned a certain area of the quilt show and are available to show the back side of quilts when people are interested. In this way, they are able to listen to the public comments without being too obvious.

Teach

Sometimes the best way to learn something is to teach it to someone else. If the student is a visual learner, a good method will be to demonstrate the technique and let the student try it in class. If the student is an audio learner, a good method will be to demonstrate and document the technique and let the student go home and try it. As a teacher, listen carefully to what the student is asking. If needed, paraphrase the question for them to be sure you really understand what they are asking.

Network

There are some quilters who have aspirations of quilting fame and strive to win national competitions. Others are satisfied by the individual artistic process and don't seek recognition. Most quilters are somewhere in between these two extremes. Similarly, most professional quilters fall somewhere between "high-priced original art" and "low-priced utilitarian stitching." By networking with other quilters, you will develop an appreciation for the niche they serve, and you will be able to find a niche that suits your talents and aspirations.

Research Your Business Idea

Most people who become professional quilters have never started their own business before. The process seems daunting because there are many things to consider. By beginning with good research, you'll be able to write a good business plan.

Professional Help

My first business proposition was to be a retail quilting studio; a place where quilters could rent time hourly on a longarm quilting machine so they could finish their quilt themselves. At the time, there were no other businesses that I could find that rented time, unless they were also a quilting machine dealer. So, I had no business model, and I needed the help of all the professionals listed below.

Most people who become professional quilters are sole proprietors (the simplest business form) working out of their own personal studio (usually in their home), and they won't need the services of everyone listed here. Although you will need some professional help, you might first need to educate the professionals regarding longarm quilting, since many don't know what it is. Develop a "business narrative" to give to the professionals so they can understand your business proposition. It is good to include photos of the machine and table.

Accountant

Find an accountant that specializes in small business to help you choose an accounting system that makes your life easier. You need to keep accurate records and prepare financial reports so you can monitor your business and comply with all financial reporting, especially taxes. With the right system, the reporting is easy. You can expect to pay several hundred dollars for the accountant's set-up help, but remember that you have the right to ask for a written estimate of the fees for doing set-up work and for any ongoing financial reporting. Each bill should document in detail what services were performed.

true story

My first accountant suggested a good accounting system but recommended too much detail (which made the bookkeeping beastly), set me up to pay monthly sales/usage tax (I now do it quarterly) and payroll tax when I didn't have any employees. Don't be afraid to speak up when talking to your accountant.

Accounting Software

Pick a system that is easy to use (so you can be quilting, not doing bookkeeping), comes with predefined financial reports (so you don't have to re-invent them), and that your accounting firm also uses (making semi-annual reviews a simple e-mail away).

Bookkeeping Detail

Avoid keeping too much detail. My rule of thumb is, if I can make a good business decision from the detail, it stays. An example is my thread inventory. My first accountant thought it would be good if I kept track of my thread so I can do an instant inventory. Sounds great, but what good is that? My current practice is to buy thread and expense it immediately, so I have no inventory. After all, it isn't like I buy thread cones so I can resell them, I just use them.

Business Type

Ask your accountant if there are advantages to any of the business types defined by your state Department of Revenue. Typical business types include: Manufacturer, Wholesaler, Retailer, Service, Agriculture, etc. Sometimes the rules are different for each type. For instance, the rules for depreciation expense (of your longarm quilting machine) are different for Manufacturers versus Services, and this might work in your favor.

Sales and Usage Tax Reporting

Sales tax is only paid by the consumer of the goods, meaning the sale of goods from manufacturer to wholesaler, and wholesaler to retailer are tax exempt. Generally the retailer sells to the consumer (there are exceptions) and must collect the sales tax and file the reports regularly. Professional quilters can buy products like thread and batting wholesale and not pay sales tax. However, since the quilter is the consumer of the thread and batting, they must pay the equivalent of the sales tax called usage tax. They must also charge sales tax on the quilting services provided and file the appropriate reports. The frequency of the reports and payments varies, so ask your accountant. Don't just agree to monthly filing. If you pay monthly (12 times) when you could be paying quarterly (four times), you are spending three times more time and effort than you have to.

tip Ask about the tax impact of hiring employees. Employee earnings are withheld for state and federal taxes, FICA, Medicare, Unemployment, etc. And, you must file the forms and pay the taxes. One alternative is to outsource your payroll tasks. Another idea is to consider hiring consultants instead of employees. You will need to file 1099 forms, but no tax withholding.

Property Tax

Each state, city and municipality has its own rules regarding property taxes. If you are required to pay property tax, look closely at the depreciation schedules for your taxable assets. For example, if you can depreciate your business computer in three to five years, and you are paying property taxes on the book value, it is beneficial for you to choose a three year depreciation schedule instead of a five year schedule because the book value goes down faster. On the other hand, if you replace your business computer in four years, and you sell the old computer for 10% of its original purchase price, you might end up paying income taxes on the gain. If your income-tax rate is greater than your property-tax rate, the net result may be a loss.

Attorney

Most professional quilters that are working at home won't need to engage an attorney, but some might consider using an attorney just to check their business plan, once they read the following text. Just like accountants, an attorney should be willing to give a written estimate of service fees.

My first business concept was to teach people to use my longarm quilting machine, and then let them rent time on an hourly basis to finish their own quilts. A big concern was the liability involved. In simple terms, if someone ran over their finger with my machine, I wasn't willing to let them sue me! So, I had my attorney draw up a release form for the customers. When I read the release, I was frightened by the terms and confused by the legal jargon. I knew I would never be willing to sign something like that, so I decided not to use the release and instead trusted that being a Limited Liability Corporation would protect my personal assets. Even though it was a wasted legal expense, I learned that business involves taking calculated risks.

Legal Entity

Sole proprietor means one person is the business. A partnership means two people are the business. There is little distinction between the business and the people. Corporations are considered separate entities, not synonymous with a person. A Limited Liability Corporation (LLC) is perhaps the simplest form of corporation, but it still requires Articles of Organization to be filed with most states. Service corporations and other corporations have more legal requirements, like filing annual meeting minutes, filing separate tax forms and being subject to different tax rules and rates. My initial business proposition allowed customers to use my equipment so it was important for me to become a limited liability corporation, and protect my retirement savings and other personal assets.

Licenses and Permits

Most professional quilters apply for a Federal Employee Identification Number (EIN) although if they are a sole proprietor, their social security number can do the same thing. Most states require each business to register for a state selling permit and/or a state sales tax exemption certificate. The forms can be filed by an individual, without the help of an attorney. The Small Business Administration (SBA) has offices in most major cities and they are a great source of help for small business owners, especially start-ups. There is a good SBA website but there are also real people in the SBA offices that are available to answer questions.

Banker

Bankers can help you choose the banking services you need, including the type of checking account, savings account, business loan, line of credit and even merchant account (for processing credit cards). The rules for the business banker are very different from the consumer banker. For instance, the banker will explain to you that businesses pay more (and differently) for checking accounts.

My bank has the best business terms in the area, but I am still required to keep a minimum balance of $2,500, I must limit the number of deposits and transfers I make, and I can only write a dozen checks or else the extra charges start to add up. I find that the number of checks written is the most difficult variable for me to control, so I now charge all my business purchases on one credit card. Therefore, I can write one check to the credit card company (for the full amount) to make the payment instead of many checks written to individual businesses.

Merchant Accounts

This type of account enables your business to accept credit cards. Your bank probably doesn't offer merchant accounts, but they can tell you the names of reputable companies. There are many merchant services available today and the costs vary significantly. The cost is determined by a flat-fee per transaction plus a percent of the transaction. Sometimes there is a monthly reporting fee. It is a good idea to compare the rates between several companies to see which are most favorable to you.

Business Loans

Business loans are available but vary widely in qualification requirements, terms and interest rates. There are grants and special loans that are available to minority-owned businesses and if you happen to be a lady, you are a minority! Take advantage of it, and check out the opportunities by comparing rates and conditions. The Small Business Administration will be able to provide you with sources for minority grants and funding. Also try contacting your local trade school to see if they have any programs. These programs are funded from federal, state and local organizations, so check them all out.

Insurance Agent

Find an agent who specializes in business policies to help you choose the right insurance coverage. Business expertise is very different from auto or residential expertise, so don't rely on your friendly homeowner policy agent. Prices vary widely, so check around.

My auto and homeowner's insurance company has great rates. When I contacted them about a business policy, I assumed that they would offer competitive rates also. Their quote seemed high so I contacted another agency that advertised being a specialist in business insurance. The second quote was half of what my homeowner's insurance company quoted. It always pays to get multiple quotes, and it doesn't cost you anything.

Business Insurance

You need business insurance even if you are in a residential location. In most cases, a homeowner's policy will not cover the cost of the longarm quilting machine or your quilting supplies, but a business policy can. If you are asked for an appraisal of you stash and supplies, call a certified quilt appraiser to help you.

Liability Insurance

Liability insurance is usually included in a business-insurance package, but not always. It covers you if you damage customer quilts, or someone has an accident on your property. The replacement value of a customer quilt is generally limited to the cost of the materials, which means it excludes the value of the time that went into making the quilt. The exception to the rule is if the quilt has already been appraised by a certified appraiser. Then it is insured for the amount of the appraisal. In most cases, customer quilts have not been appraised. There is a special type of insurance coverage called Bailees Coverage. It was designed for insuring works of art in a gallery setting and requires an appraisal of each piece. Bailees coverage is not needed by most professional quilters, but if you do have a studio that doubles as an art gallery when you display customer quilts, you might want to look into it.

Realtor

When I was looking for a commercial location, I found a suitable location and contacted the realtor that was handling the property. He showed me the property and gave me a copy of the lease. I didn't find the lease reasonable even though I was told that the terms were standard. I made a copy of the lease, made the changes that I thought were reasonable and gave it to my attorney for final legal wording. I asked for a reduction in the rent, a limit to the annual increase (COLA), a buy-out clause after one year, and asked that the owner make some changes to the property to make it more suitable for my business. When I told the realtor that I had a counter lease, he said it was unreasonable and kept me from talking to the property owner. I refused to take no for an answer and waited several weeks, until the owner was available. The terms of my counter lease were accepted by the owner, and we were able to come to an agreement.

Suppliers

Find a sewing supply distributor that handles longarm quilting supplies. Not all do! If possible, develop a good relationship with the customer service representative that handles your account. This person is a good source for marketing research information, especially knowing what is hot and what is not!

Wholesale Purchases

Buying wholesale usually means you will pay 45-50% of what the retail value is for the items. This sounds great, but keep in mind that lots of extra rules and charges apply. There are minimum-order quantities which means buying "one" means buying one box or case, not one unit. With fabric, you will be buying a bolt rather than a yard of fabric. Expect to have a minimum-order value of at least $100, and if you don't meet that minimum, plan on being charged a handling fee. Also plan on paying shipping, and don't be surprised if there is an additional surcharge for deliveries to residential locations. Oversized items refer to anything large, bulky or heavy and will cost extra for shipping too.

Batting

Buying batting on a roll instead of individual packages is usually more cost effective. It comes in different widths (my favorite is the 94" queen-size width). Shipping companies have limits to the size of shippable packages, so batting is usually folded in half before being shipped. Puffy batting can be folded after it is wrapped on the roll, but flat batting is usually folded in half before it is wrapped on the roll. Either way, be prepared to pay extra shipping charges because it is considered oversized.

Initial Order

The best time to open an account with a supplier is when you are first setting up your business. Sometimes suppliers will have special discounts or payment terms (delaying the invoice due date for 30-60 days) that are designed to help a new business get going. Usually, these special incentives apply only to the first order. Plan your first order so you know you are getting everything you need, but don't be tempted to buy enough to last a year. You are investing in the raw materials you need, but you don't want to commit all your cash.

Customer Service Policies

Always ask about the policies. Specifically, ask about backorders. Will you be told when you are placing the order if something is going to be backordered? If you don't accept back-orders (this means you prefer to cancel any item that would be on backorder, and try to find it somewhere else), will your minimum-order value be affected? If you do accept backorders, will you have to pay shipping on the portion of the order that was backor-dered? If you need to return an item, what is the return policy? Most companies charge a 15% restocking fee on returns unless the mis-take was theirs. If they made the mistake, the return will have to be pre-authorized, so ask what the procedure is.

Summary

The final decisions are yours! Don't let the details scare you, just find the professionals you need for your business proposition, and start asking questions. When you have the right information, the decisions will be much easier to make. Remember that each state has different rules regarding business opera-tions so the experiences listed here are just an outline of what might be appropriate for your business in your state.

Business Plan

The terms "business plan," "financial plan," "marketing plan" and other plans all add up to being an intimidating barrier to your new beginning, but don't let that stop you. Your business plan can be a single page or whole book. You decide, it's your plan!

All plans have similar characteristics, and they force you to commit to paper all the great ideas that are floating around in your cre-ative brain! The bigger the business, the more details to consider. So for most of us, a simple business plan will work fine. By actually writ-ing down the details, you will be able to see where you have gaps and overlaps in your plan. By including a timeline and benchmarks, you will be able to track your progress.

Company Background

What are your credentials? This is the place where you document the reasons why you can run a successful business. Include how your past experiences have prepared you for this step, how much money you can afford to in-vest, how much time you will be spending, and how it will fit into your lifestyle.

Goals

What are your personal and professional goals? How will you know when you achieve those goals? What does success look like? If you can't define what you consider success you might not realize how successful you are! Success does not have to be measured monetarily. It could be developing a solid reputation in the quilting com-munity or incorporating artistic expression into your lifestyle or some other definition.

Products/Services

What specifically will you offer? Start with the primary focus (probably professional-quilting services to individuals), but include any ancillary products you can offer (like binding services, etc). Be sure to include how it delivers value to your customers.

Target Customers

Who are the people that you want as customers? Be sure to identify who are they, what they want, how you satisfy them, and what they will pay. This part will require some marketing research, which can also be a lot of fun. If possible, document the different ways you will be in contact with your target customers (see page 113). For example, you will contact target customers when you are at a quilt guild meeting, teaching a class, taking a class, shopping at your quilt shop, entering quilt shows, etc. What can you do at each contact to promote your business?

Logistics

How are you going to get all of this done? Identify how you will meet with your customers, discuss what needs to be done, how you will do the quilting, deliver the finished quilt and get paid. By writing all this down, you will be identifying all the details that need to be considered like business hours, credit-card payments, invoices, worksheets, refund policies, etc. This is the place where you define your customer-service level, and make sure you can meet it.

Timeline

Set a reasonable timeline for your plans. Break down your goals into attainable steps and estimate how much time they will take. You might be surprised at how long it takes to get a new business up and running. If possible, seek input from other professional quilters and ask what lessons they learned along the way. See if they think your timeline is reasonable. Use the timeline to check on your progress. Celebrate your successes and don't get discouraged by those rude life-lessons we sometimes stumble upon.

Marketing Plan

The five principles of marketing are product, price, promotion, place and people. There are really only four "P" principles, but I added people, because people are so important in the quilting community.

Marketing is all about positioning. How does your product compare to others? The factors for this comparison are the five principles of marketing. Every company needs to define their product, set the pricing policies, promote the product to increase awareness, deliver the product and put the people in place to get it all done. Normally, companies excel at one principle so they focus on it, and use it to differentiate themselves from others.

Product

Define your product in terms of quality, innovation and style. If your product is your quilting style, make sure you are an expert at that style and charge accordingly. Never agree to use a technique that you are not familiar with, the risks are too high. Know when to turn down business or refer a quilt to some other quilter.

Price

Pricing is much more than a fee. The price you charge reflects your quilting fees less any coupons, discounts, free supplies or free services you provided. This amount should cover all your costs which might include a portion of the rent, utilities, office equipment, quilting equipment costs, raw materials, inventory costs, and labor and administrative costs. And the price should leave you some extra which is your profit.

Promotion

Raising awareness so the customer will call you when they need your services is a result of promotions. Advertising, web sites, referral programs and even show and tell at your local quilt guild help raise awareness. Promoting your business needs to be a continuous effort. Public relations announcements and press releases are usually free, so try to interest your newspaper to write something about your business. You will need to pay for advertising, so choose a media that finds your target audience. Local newspaper is rarely the best media.

Place

(Also called distribution.) Being at the right place at the right time is usually not an accident. For professional quilting, the right place at the right time means being available. Convenient location, flexible hours and quick turnaround time are examples of being in the right place at the right time.

People

People are not traditionally one of the marketing Ps, but people are so important. The customer has put a lot of time and money into their quilt tops, and they need to trust the person who will finish it. You have the equipment and skill to complete the quilt, but they had the original vision, so listen to what their vision is and interpret it the best way possible. A customer can be disappointed when the finished quilt does not look like the vision, even though the workmanship was good and the price was fair.

Ideas for Your Marketing Plan

Most marketing plans identify where the business is today, where the business is headed and what the plan is to get there. They typically start by defining the overall marketing message and then modifying the message to suit free publicity, paid advertising, web-site development, literature development, and a schedule of activities like shows, classes and conferences.

• Develop your marketing message. Pick your strength and use it to differentiate your business from the competition. Be sure to phrase your message so it defines the benefits you provide and how those benefits equate to customer value.

• Schedule promotions. If at all possible, design your promotions so you can measure the cost of executing the promotion and the amount of incremental business you gained from it.

• Design a promotion to gain new business. A "First-Timers" coupon is a good way to drum up new business.

• Find ways to strengthen the customer relationship by reminding the customer of who you are and what you do. Example: Design a calendar that lists all the quilt-related activities going on in your area. Make the calendar so attractive that customers and shops will post it on their bulletin board. Have your business name, number and web site prominently displayed.

• Generate regular newsletters to maintain customer awareness. The newsletters can promote new patterns, skills or techniques that you now offer. Remind your customers of the extra services you can offer, like preparing the quilt backing, binding, etc. It should also advertise your promotional events.

• Develop promotions to fill in the slow times during the year. Example: For each quilt done between November and December, earn 15% off quilting done in January and February.

• Have a quilt show. If you have the room, find a mini-group (or quilting bee) that is too small to have their own quilt shows. Make it like an art-gallery event, with a program listing each quilt, each quilter, etc. Include food and drink if appropriate. Take pictures of all quilts. Send thank-you notes to each participant.

• Design a program to strengthen customer loyalty, perhaps a "Thanks for the Referral" coupon giving a 15% discount on the next quilt. Be sure your discount is significant to be memorable.

Prepare a Publicity Campaign

> **tip** The difference between publicity and marketing is that publicity is usually free.

• Notify newspapers of the events you plan and host (like the mini-group shows).

• Distribute flyers at quilt guilds, quilt shows, quilt shops, local and regional museums, art shops, tourist areas, city convention centers, theaters, or other shops that cater to the same demographics.

• Write an article about some topic that you do well and submit it to various magazines.

• Be generous and offer to quilt the first several quilts donated to a charity.

• Search the Internet and get your name on any appropriate directories.

Prepare an Advertising Campaign

> **tip** Advertising is rarely free.

• Advertise your services in the newsletters of local / regional guilds.

• Advertise your services in the newsletters of your local / regional quilt shops.

• Do a magazine ad (can be expensive, classified ads in magazines are less expensive.)

• Advertise in newsletters of organizations that appeal to similar demographics, like museums or art galleries.

> **tip** Pull out your business and marketing plans from time to time to evaluate your progress. Be honest, ask for input where appropriate and don't be too hard on yourself. Revise your plans annually.

Thank your customers.

Build a Good Reputation

A good reputation is built gradually. It consists of other people's opinions of your skills, the value of your quilting and your attitude.

Develop your personal skills by taking classes, attending shows, doing charity quilts, taking and studying photos, and, of course, practicing. Never offer a service unless you are sure you can execute it well.

Develop your interpersonal skills by networking with your guild(s), shop(s), teacher(s), and other associations. Join the guild and then offer to take a position on the board. Don't use these positions to solicit business. Offer to teach a class. Again, don't sell your services, just sell yourself as a knowledgeable (and nice) quilter.

Develop your professional reputation by being professional in every target customer contact. Customer contacts include:

•Meeting people who might become your customers.

•Meeting people who bring you a quilt.

•Meeting people when they pick up a quilt (never belittle yourself).

•People asking for suggestions on how to improve some technique. (Don't offer! Wait for them to ask.)

•Talking to people about other quilters. (NEVER bad mouth anyone else.)

•Support your local quilt shop. Don't discount any fabric or batting they sell.

•Support your local guilds and teachers. This is a community, not a competition.

•Show appreciation to your customers. Send personal notes when appropriate, especially for referrals.

Your First Customer

You've planned and you've practiced, and you're finally ready to accept your first customer. Chances are it will be a friend or family member, but you still need to be ready with your price list, your quilting worksheet and your camera!

What to Charge?

When setting prices it is wise to consider every supply you provide and every task you do to prepare for, execute and finish the quilting job. In addition, you have overhead costs (like your computer or quilting machine) that you need and must pay for.

Supplies you might be providing:
•Batting
•Thread
•Special Purchases

Tasks you might be performing:

tip You can and should charge for these tasks: cleaning, winding bobbins, threading, pinning on, positioning, basting, binding, ironing clipping stray threads, trimming, adding framing strips, washing and drying fabric, binding, etc.

•Initial customer interview
•Machine setup
•Loading the quilt
•Time spent quilting
•Quilt Top Preparation
  •Backing preparation
  •Turning the quilt
   (if needed for side borders)
  •Hand tied knots and thread burying
  •Stencil marking and mark removal
  •Original pattern design
•Binding
•Customer pick-up appointment

Overhead Costs

tip

Administrative tasks include: ordering, paying bills, balancing accounts, figuring taxes and payments, etc.

- Administrative tasks
- Credit Card processing
- Business banking services
- Business insurance costs
- Rent and utilities (even if your studio is in your home)
- Office supplies
- Computer and software expenses
- Quilting machine expense and any other equipment
- Inventory carrying costs

Marketing Research

There are many things to consider when setting your pricing, but none is as important as knowing what the competition is charging. If your customers are local (they come to your studio), your competition is probably located in a 50 mile radius. If you will be using your web site as your studio (meaning you have customers send their quilt tops to you), your target market could be anywhere in the world, but it is most likely within your home country. Do some marketing research and find out what others are charging. Include quilting fees *plus* any extra fees. Many professional quilters have brochures or business cards available at fabric shops. A serious competitor will also have a web site and take credit-card payments. Check out their web sites and set a competitive price for your services. If you have chosen to differentiate yourself based on price, you should be as low or lower than the others. If you differentiate yourself with high quality or fast turn-around time, your prices can be higher.

Methods for Setting Prices

Most quilters I know use size as their pricing basis, meaning they quote a price that is dependent on the size of the quilt top. That price covers the cost of the overhead and all the tasks performed, the only extras are the supplies provided. Different size measurements (inch, foot, yard) can be equated:

Price per square inch = Price per square foot $\div 144$ = Price per square yard $\div 1296$

Others prefer a menu pricing, meaning they can't give a quote until the worksheet is complete and each task is assigned a fee. Quilters who specialize in custom quilting use this method most commonly.

Still others use time as their pricing basis. Nationally recognized quilters who specialize in show quality quilting often use this pricing method.

When comparing your pricing structure to others, be sure to calculate the real bottom-line price.

Worksheet Estimate

I have developed a custom-quilting services worksheet that I use to record all my notes from the customer interview and to provide a written cost estimate to my customers. I am including it here, and I encourage you to copy and use the worksheet if you feel it works for you.

When I meet a customer for the first time, I describe what happens at our initial meeting, and I explain that they get a written estimate that I will honor for 30 days. They don't have to leave the quilt with me immediately, especially if they have agreed to do some of the prep work like trimming threads, adding framing strips or ironing. When they leave my studio, they have a copy of the worksheet that both of us have signed and dated.

tip Special charges and totals are not computed until after the quilting is done. My worksheet has evolved over time and yours will, too. If you would like to use any part of my worksheet, please do!

The Customer Interview

You can learn a lot about your customer by explaining the worksheet and answering their questions. One of the most important questions you will ask is "What is our budget?" This question will help you suggest quilting designs that are within the budget.

•Relate to them on their level. Are they artists or engineers?

•Be easy to do business with. Talk business, but include a little personal time. Let them get to know you (and try to get to know them).

•Be Professional. Keep your studio organized. Listen carefully to what customers say. If they ask for a design or technique you have not yet mastered, be honest and say so. Even suggest that they take the quilt to someone else who is capable or offer an alternative solution.

•Market yourself. Remind the customer that you offer more than just quilting. If you know they don't like to do something like binding, offer to do it for them (for a fee).

•Be the expert. Make up some information sheets that describe "How To" directions for various tasks like borders, bindings, and hanging sleeves. Share them when appropriate.

•Be appreciative. Thank them for their business! Take two sets of photos of the quilt you just completed and send a set to your customer in a thank-you note that says you appreciate their trust. (Put the other one in your own scrap book, which you can also use to help demonstrate your skills to other new customers).

tip If you make a suggestion and the customer says, "OK," but their expression is uncomfortable, make another suggestion and discuss the choices until they are smiling.

tip When I photograph customer quilts, at least one picture has the quilt draped on the table of the quilting machine, and the quilting machine is visible. Not many people have seen a longarm machine and by including it in your photo, your customer can explain longarm quilting to friends and family.

Custom Quilting Services

Name:_____

E-mail address:_____

Address:_____

City, State, Zip: _____

Phone: (H)   _____

     (W)   _____

     (C)   _____

Quilting Description:

Dates:
Quote done_____   Promised_____

Completed _____   Show Entry? (Yes / No)

Have fabrics been washed ?   (Yes / No)
Finish Knots by hand/machine? _____
Marking preferences? _____

Quilt Top Size: (inches) _____x_____

Backing Size: (inches) _____x_____

Cost Estimate:
Quilting: _____   _____

Thread: _____   _____

Batting: _____   _____

Backing: _____   _____

Binding: _____   _____

Special Charges:

Apply framing strips	_____	
Turning charge	_____	
Thread changes	_____	
Final Trim/square charge	_____	
Pattern Purchase	_____	
Other _____	_____	
Total Special Charges	_____	

Special Chg _____

Subtotal _____

Sales Tax _____

Total: =========

Less Deposit _____

Plus Shipping _____

Total Due: =========

I authorize the work listed above. I understand that the figures are only estimates of the costs and I am financially responsible for the final cost of services rendered and supplies provided by _____. _____ is not bound to the approximate completion date listed above.

Estimate Provided by: _____ Date: _____

Accepted by: _____ Date: _____
        (Customer Signature)

Skill Builders

It is a good idea to practice free motion and pantograph quilting on a practice quilt. Load the machine with a couple yards of plain fabric (both quilt top and backing). Add batting and you have a practice quilt!

Begin with free-motion quilting. Practicing the styles in the order listed will help build confidence. Start with meandering loops, add stars, try to stipple, stitch some leaves and swirls, and finally do some echo stitching. Time spent mastering each style will help you gain the control you will need when you advance to stencils and more complicated free motion techniques.

Continue practicing by doing pantographs. Two full-size patterns are included. The simple meander pattern is the easiest. The flower pattern is more difficult, but more flexible.

Simple Meander Pattern

•Resize the pattern if needed to the desired scale.

•Copy the resized pattern as many times as needed to span the width of the practice quilt.

•Trim or fold the copies as needed so the 'Repeat Start' point of one joins the 'Repeat End' point of the previous one. Tape together if desired.

•Position the pattern pieces under the plastic sheet on the table, using the registration marks to keep them straight.

•Align the pattern to the quilt

Be sure to complete several rows of the meandering pattern before moving on to more complicated patterns.

Flower Pattern — Straight Set

The flower pattern can be stitched edge-to-edge (E2E) like the Simple Meander pattern. The straight set is shown on page 121. It can also be staggered (see Staggered Set) for added interest. To stitch the flower pattern in a straight set, follow the same directions as the Simple Meander: Resize, copy, trim, position pattern, align quilt and stitch.

Flower Pattern — Staggered Set

To stitch the flower pattern in a staggered set you will need to align the second row differently and modify the pattern somewhat. Here is what to consider:

•Align the first pattern row to your quilt as described in the directions.

•Find and mark the current row entry point.

•Find the next row entry point which will be up and sideways.

•If the next row entry point is off the quilt, modify the side pattern (first repeat of the second row) however needed to keep the stitching on the quilt. For this pattern that means marking half a flower for half of a repeat.

•Modify the other side (last repeat of the second row) pattern also.

•Always check the positioning before stitching. This means moving the machine without stitching to check that the new row won't have too much space (big gap) or too little space (overlap) between rows.

Simple Meander Pattern

Repeat Start

Repeat End

Flower Pattern

Repeat Start

Repeat End

Flower Pattern — Staggered Set

Use the dashed line for designing staggered rows

About the Author

Pat Barry opened her longarm quilting studio, Quilter's Studio, LLC, in 2002. After taking a preliminary class, many of her customers rent time on her machines. Through her business, Pat has had the opportunity to teach over 250 people how to use her longarm quilting machine.

Pat belongs to many quilt guilds and professional organizations. She works with Quilt Center, LLC, a leading Gammill Quilting System Dealer as a trainer and as an authorized Gammill sales representative. Working with Quilt Center allows Pat to attend all the major trade shows, and it has given her the chance to interact and teach the whole range of longarm quilters, from those who are thinking of buying a machine to those who have owned a machine for years. Her popular pre-ownership clinics for The Quilt Center are always insightful and entertaining.

Pat conducts workshops, presentations and classes on longarm quilting topics around the country.

Pat would like to thank John and Sabrina Karlen and the staff at The Quilt Center for letting her use the facility to shoot photographs for this book. She would also like to thank Marcia Rhone for opening her delightful Clear Pond Quilting Studio as an additional photography location.

Resources

Machines and Quilting Supplies

The Quilt Center, LLC
1905 Center Ave
Janesville, WI 53546
Sales: 1-877-needles
Service 608-756-2869

Golden Threads
Patterns and notions
245 W. Roosevelt Road, Suite 61
West Chicago, IL 60185
Sales: 1-888-477-7718
Office: 630-231-2800

Gammill Quilting Systems
1452 W. Gibson St.
West Plains, MO 65775
417-256-5919
1-800-659-8224

By Design Quilting, LLC
Books, zippers and accessories
Al and Pat Barry
5640 Tracy Circle
Racine, WI 53402
262-681-2000

Professional Associations

International Machine Quilters Association
(IMQA)
P.O. Box 6647
Monona, WI 53716
www.IMQA.org

International Quilt Association (IQA)
7660 Woodway Drive Suite 550
Houston, TX 77063
www.Quilts.org

National Quilting Association (NQA)
P.O. Box 12190
Columbus, OH 43212
www.NQAQuilts.org

American Quilting Society (AQS)
P.O. Box 3290
Paducah, KY 42002
www.AmericanQuilter.com

Wisconsin Quilters Inc (WQI)
P.O. Box 2471
Brookfield, WI 53008
www.wisconsinquilters.com

Publications

The Professional Quilter: The Business
Journal for Serious Quilters
22412 Rolling Hill Lane
Laytonsville, MD 20882
www.professionalquilter.com

SQE Professional (Sewing, Quilting,
Embroidery) Magazine
By VDTA/SDTA, 2724 2nd Ave.
Des Moines, IA 50313
www.vdta.com

CNA: Turning Creative Ideas into Profits
F+W Publications
4700 E. Galbraith Rd.
Cincinnati, OH 45236
www.cnamag.com

On Track! A Magazine for Professional
Machine Quilters
Published by International Machine Quilters
Association (See above)

The Quilting Quarterly
Published by National Quilting Association
(See above)

American Quilter Magazine
Published by American Quilting Society
(See above)

Showtime Quilters Guide & Directory:
Quilters Helping Quilters
P.O. Box 13567
Spokane, WA 99213
1-800-854-9239
www.Quiltershelpingquilters.com

Professional Longarm Yellowbook: A piecer's
resource guide to machine quilters
2724 2nd Ave.
Des Moines, IA 50313
www.quiltingprofessional.com

Quilters Traveling Companion
32 Grand Ave.
Manitou Springs, CO 80829
www.chalet-publishing.com

Discussion Groups

The Longarm List
www.Quiltropolis.com

Machine Quilting Professionals
www.yahoo/groups

Quilt Shows

Innovations
MQInnovations.com

Original Sewing & Quilting Expo
SewingExpo.com

Greater Chicago Quilt Expo
Schaumburg, IL
Quiltfest.com

International Quilt Festival
Quilts.com

MQX Machine Quilters Expo
MQXShow.com

Home Machine Quilting Show
HMQS.org

AQS Annual Convention
Paducah, KY
AmericanQuilter.com

International Quilt Market
Quilts.com

MQS Machine Quilters Showcase
IMQA.org

NQA Annual show
NQAQuilts.org

Minnesota Quilt Show
St. Paul, MN
MNQuilt.org

AQS Expo
AmericanQuilter.com

Quilt Expo
Madison, WI
WIquiltexpo.com
Additional Resources

Other Resources

Annie's Attic
1 Annie Lane
Big Sandy, TX 75755
Phone: 800-582-6643
Web: www.anniesattic.com

Clotilde LLC
P.O. Box 7500
Big Sandy, TX 75755-7500
Phone: 800-772-2891
Web: www.clotilde.com

Connecting Threads
P.O. Box 870760
Vancouver, WA 98687-7760
Phone: 800-574-6454
Web: www.ConnectingThreads.com

Ghee's
2620 Centenary Blvd. No. 2-250
Shreveport, LA 71104
Phone: 318-226-1701
E-mail: bags@ghees.com
Web: www.ghees.com

Herrschners, Inc.
2800 Hoover Road
Stevens Point, WI 54492-0001
Phone: 800-441-0838
Web: www.herrschners.com/

Home Sew
P.O. Box 4099
Bethlehem, PA 18018-0099
Phone: 800-344-4739
Web: www.homesew.com

Keepsake Quilting
Route 25
P.O. Box 1618
Center Harbor, NH 03226-1618
Phone: 800-438-5464
Web: www.keepsakequilting.com

Krause Publications
700 E. State St.
Iola WI 54990
Phone: 800-258-0929
Web: www.krausebooks.com

Nancy's Notions
333 Beichl Ave.
P.O. Box 683
Beaver Dam, WI 53916-0683
Phone: 800-833-0690
Web: www.nancysnotions.com

Take Your Quilting Skills to a New Level

Chameleon Quilts
*Versatile Looks
Using Traditional Patterns*

by Margrit Hall,
Foreword by Earlene Fowler

Learn how to use new fabrics, colors and textures and the same set of 10 quilt patterns to create 19 different projects. Features more than 200 step-by-step color photos and graphics.

Softcover • 8¼ x 10⅞
128 pages • 200+ color photos
Item# Z0104 • $22.99

Quilt As Desired
*Your Guide to Straight-Line and
Free-Motion Quilting*

by Charlene C. Frable

Let this revolutionary guide help you expand your skills, with instructions for straight-line and free-motion techniques. Discover what it means to truly quilt as desired.

Hardcover • 8¼ x 10⅞
128 pages • 150 color photos
Item# Z0743 • $24.99

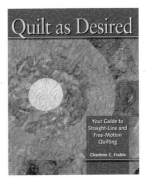

The Civil War Love Letter Quilt
*121 Quilt Blocks
Inspired by Love and War*

by Rosemary Youngs

Third in a unique series of historical letter and quilt books, this guide features 121 different paper-pieced block patterns, and related letters. All the block patterns in this book are interchangeable with those in the other books of the series.

Softcover • 8 x 8 • 288 pages
20 color photos, 300 color illus.
Item# Z0751 • $22.99

The Art of Landscape Quilting

by Nancy Zieman
and Natalie Sewell

This one-stop resource includes instructions for 16 upscale step-by-step projects and 20 partial projects; complete with tips, tricks and techniques for successfully designing and completing landscape quilts.

Softcover • 10 x 7 • 144 pages
200 color photos
Item# LQCG • $24.99

Bundles of Fun
Quilts From Fat Quarters

by Karen Snyder

Discover fabric selection advice, instructions for making smaller quilts and adding borders, all in this one book. Offers variations for 12 coordinating projects.

Softcover • 8¼ x 10⅞
128 pages • 150+ color photos and illus.
Item# FQLQ • $22.99